Career
Transition

make the shift

Your 5 Steps to Successful Career Reinvention

Deborah Shane

Career Transition - Make the Shift
Your 5 Steps to Successful Career Reinvention
Deborah Shane

Advanced Praise

*"Nobody cares as deeply as Deborah Shane.
Get her on your side."*
Tory Johnson, founder of Women for Hire, ABC Good Morning America contributor, best-selling author

"Deborah's book is a comprehensive guide to career transition and reinvention, in a time of great change and shift. She draws on her own career evolution as well as the opportunity and influence women have now to step out and step up to having the career of their dreams!"
Maddy Dychtwald, author of "Influence: How Women's Soaring Economic Power Will Transform Our World for the Better," co-founder & senior vice president of Age Wave

"This 'take action' book approach inspired by true stories and experiences will help you look inside and out, dig deep and pull out the career path that you are truly passionate about and should be actively transitioning to or living every single day."
Starr Hall, international speaker, best-selling author, starrhall.com

"One of the things I always look for as a journalist is someone who can do more than just talk about lofty ideas. I want the who, what, when, where, why and how. Deborah does that, in a clear and insightful way. If you

want to get started on your new career path, Deborah should be your trusted GPS."
Anita Bruzzese, syndicated columnist for Gannett/USAToday.com

"If you're currently in career transition, if you've recently lost your job, or if you're committed to the process of figuring out 'what's next' in your career .... then you've got to read Deborah Shane's newest book, 'Career Transition: Make the Shift.' Drawing upon her own personal experience in successfully navigating a total shift in career direction, and incorporating her gifts of coaching and training others, Deborah provides a well-thought-out, practical and holistic process for anyone embarking upon a career change or considering a shift in career direction. Excellent work Deborah! I highly recommend the book and as well as the accompanying workbook."
Andy Robinson, Executive Career Coach, CEO - CRG Leadership Institute LLC

"Deborah is experienced, passionate and never boring. She constantly updates her training materials to reflect current economic, cultural and business trends. One of Deborah's many strong points is her ability to engage all participants in the training process. She has the gift of helping people feel comfortable in her presence right from the beginning. Even shy people will often participate with Deborah's engaging methodology."
Nancy Smith, Coordinator of the Lee County School District Business and Industry Services

"Deborah is a gifted educator. Her book debunks the age old saying, "You can't teach an old dog new tricks." This is a must read for anyone wanting to learn how to make the transition. From start to finish, this powerful book guides you toward finding your path to happiness and success from a "Master Educator and Motivator," Deborah Shane."
Barry Gottlieb, Author, Speaker, Trusted Advisor

"If you're not satisfied with your career today, arm yourself with this book!"
Anita Campbell, CEO of SmallBizTrends.com

Career Transition - Make the Shift
Your 5 Steps to Successful Career Reinvention
by Deborah Shane

Copyright ©2010 by Deborah Shane. All rights reserved.

ISBN: 1452819939

ISBN -13: 9781452819938

Book and Cover Design: Tom Messina of TotalConcepts.com

Printed in the United States of America

*The answer lies within ourselves.
If we can't find peace and happiness there,
it's not going to come from the outside.*
—Tenzin Palmo, Tibetan Buddhist

To all the teachers that saw a spark in me and always encouraged me to kindle my mind and spirit.

To the many friends and colleagues that have journeyed with me, walking in the right direction, to somewhere.

To my father, Martin, who passed away when I was only twenty-six. Somehow, he knew that the guitar and the equipment he bought me for my first band, as well as the conversations on the beach about life's disappointments, would be the cherished memories of a relationship cut short.

To my mother, Ruth, for her adventuresome, curious, and fun-loving spirit. I will always remember her words, "You only come this way one time, so try it and do it now."

To my brothers Jeff and Glenn, who are my best friends, and who love and support me no matter what!

Special thanks to Alysia Shivers for helping me bring this dream together and to fruition with your insight, input, and patience.

Forward

When you think about all the hours we spend working, it's easy to see how we can dread the idea of having to change gears. In our minds, we see each hour as a brick in a 'career house' we are constructing. The time and energy we put forth is our professional sweat equity. So, when unexpected job loss or the sudden need to shift career directions occurs, it can feel like we are walking away from a half-built home. The disappointment can be great, and the fear of losing the warmth and protection from what we built can be unnerving.

The pages in this book are designed to help you see that you aren't starting over, but rather, altering your home's design. Deborah Shane is a career architect that will help you see the possibilities. Her energy, insight and practical guidance will help you recognize that you have a foundation from which a hundred career masterpieces can be constructed.

I still remember my first interaction with Deborah. She invited me on to her popular Internet radio show. I'd had the pleasure to be interviewed on various career shows plenty of times before, but this was the first time where I forgot I was being interviewed! Deborah engaged me in a conversation that was so positive and fun - it was as if she had been able to read my mind. As you work through this book, I feel certain you will have a similar experience. Deborah has used her strengths as an empowerment expert and her own career reinvention experiences to help you find the confidence and courage to pursue your career on your own terms.

I wish you the best in your journey to find greater career satisfaction. I guarantee Deborah's book and companion Career Action Book will inspire you to keep building the career of your dreams!

J.T. O'Donnell
Founder/President, Careerealism.com

Preface

I am a tenacious woman who has transitioned through several careers.

My career path has taken me into the corporate and entrepreneurial worlds a few times over. In 2006, I made a decision to change my entire life as I had known it over the past twenty-five years! I wasn't laid off or downsized. I wasn't fired (thankfully). I made a thoughtful, voluntary decision to change my career path and continue my life in a new direction. In February 2007, I officially became an entrepreneur for the second time. That decision was a two-year process. It was the right time and the right decision for me.

I have met many people forced into a career transition that they didn't see coming. Many of them are educated professionals that worked at jobs they thought they would be at forever. They are now unemployed or dissatisfied with their current work life and wondering what's next and how to get there.

My story and the process I went through are a testimony that career transition is a beginning and an adventure. Our lives do not go vertical or horizontal. Our lives meander like a stream.

When I embraced change and the process it takes to change like an adventure, things started happening. I started to have fun. Yes, fun living it out! It is the most exciting and challenging thing I have done, but the payoff is, and will be, worth it. To be the master of your destiny and life, to be able to use your talents and gifts to better others, is a fascinating journey. Not everyone is cut out to do it, but if it's something you want and you believe you have the qualities to do, than it is only as far as your willingness to do it!

This book is my story, my process, and the lessons I've learned, as well as examples of other women who have reinvented, re-branded, and re-birthed themselves and their lives to live in their passion and purpose. It is my hope that my story inspires and motivates women and men of any age to believe that the life they want is the life they can have. It takes vision, guts, hard work, support, flexibility, and perseverance.

It is an honor and a privilege to do what I do. When you can combine your vocation with what you love, it is the ultimate opportunity to create a lasting legacy. It is a process that anyone can experience; you just have to get started. There is no overnight success in life. Look at any successful entrepreneur, big or small. Each one started with an idea, a spark, and a belief that he could better himself and others.

I've lived and worked in southeast Florida since I was ten years old. My career path has been a journey combining education, entertainment, sales, and marketing. I spent over twenty years in broadcast radio in the Miami/Ft. Lauderdale area, but I yearned for something more out of my professional life. I sought a new adventure, which brought me to southwest Florida in August 2006, but an unexpected series of circumstances forced me to alter my plans. It was a Thursday afternoon about 3 p.m. when I answered the question, "What do you really want to do, not what do you have to do?"

I launched my third business, Train with Shane, in February 2007. Today, I dedicate myself to people who want or need to make similar lifestyle and career changes. I am an empowerment advocate, assisting people in their professional development to strengthen their business skills, their self-esteem, their confidence, and their personal brand.

To find your new path and create a great new reality for your life, I'll be referring to the following four keys to transitioning:

• Everything you need is already inside of you.

• Transition is another beginning and a new adventure.

• Adapt and apply who you already are and what you do best to your now.

• What it looks like is what it looks like today.

Here's my story.

It could be your story, too.

Part One-My Story

Never stop because you are afraid—you
are never so likely to be wrong.
—Fridtjof Nansen (1861-1930),
Norwegian explorer/Nobel Peace Prize winner

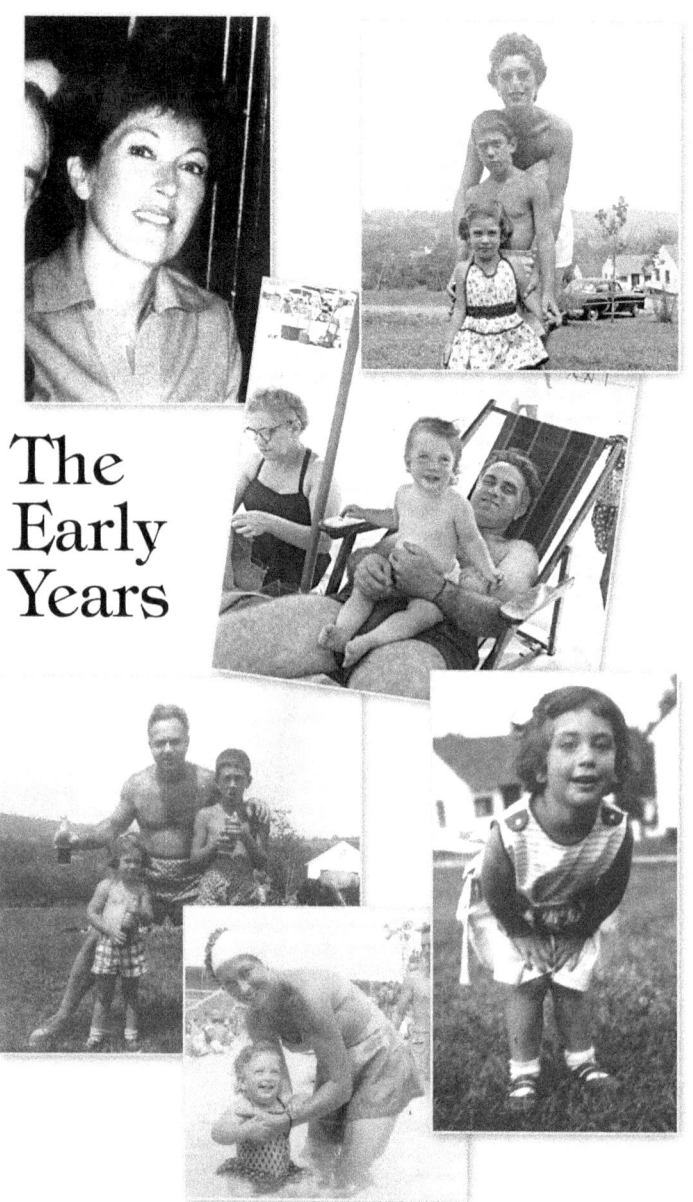

The
Early
Years

Chapter 1

Childhood Shapers and Turning Points

*I'm youth, I'm joy, I'm a little bird that
has broken out of the egg.*
**—James Barrie (1860–1937),
Scottish author and dramatist**

The paths we take in life are an adventurous, meandering journey. Like any adventure, they are full of twists, turns, curves, potholes, darkness, fog, and brilliant sunlight. They unfold and seem to become more meaningful as we journey through them. They have a beginning, middle, and an ongoing. They always lead to where we are supposed to go.

My life's journey has been an adventure because I have an adventuresome spirit. I love to explore, learn new things, and meet new people. I welcome a lot of input and stimulation, which fuels my love for learning and sharing.

My mother, Ruth, taught me about being curious and adventuresome. She always encouraged me to try things. She was one of the biggest influences on my life, and she had a great impact on me. She, too, had that adventuresome spirit, but didn't get to take advantage of it until she was in her fifties. After my father passed away in 1978 at the age sixty-two, my mom took off on many trips and side journeys to try things, meet new people, and discover new places. She went on a Greyhound bus tour from Florida to California with my aunt Molly. She was curious, she was open-minded, and she always helped people. She passed all that on to me.

My dad, Martin, came from a divorced home and grew up with a single working mom, which back then was *not* the norm. His father was abusive in many ways, and my father brought a lot of that dysfunction into his own family. He yelled a lot. I had a few major head butts with him when I was a kid, but I also know he loved me. (His relationship with me was different from those that he had with my brothers, because I was his little girl.) After the divorce of his parents, he had to work to help the family survive. He was responsible, a hard worker, a man of his word, kindhearted, and frugal. He passed most of that on to me. I developed an "overachiever thing" with him, which I hoped would make him yell and criticize less. It eventually did, and it uncovered in me a strong need to achieve. I *love* a challenge. It fuels me big time.

Family

I was born in Manhattan, New York, on July 8. My mom and dad were ecstatic that they had their little girl. My brother Jeff was three years older than me. Seven years later, my younger brother Glenn was born. I lived in Forrest Hills, Queens, New York, the first nine years of my life. It was a nice neighborhood with Austin Park just down the street.

Though I was a shy child, I was active. I didn't like being too far from my family, and yet I loved going to Austin Park where I could participate in sports and other outdoor activities.

I started playing guitar, singing, and writing songs and lyrics when I was eight. These were powerful gifts and talents that allowed me to express my creativity and to shape my self-image. Music was a world I could go to that brought me great joy and self-esteem. I spent hours in my room, practicing, singing, and performing for myself.

When I was eight, my father, only forty-four at the time, had a mild heart attack. A couple of years after that, he decided the cold New York weather was not healthful for him anymore, and he moved us to Miami Beach, Florida. I was scared, but at the same time excited and curious because it was a new adventure. At that time, Miami had not yet exploded culturally and ethnically, and it was a small, homogenous family and vacation town.

Sports, music, adventure, curiosity, challenge ... these were my first *shapers and turning points* as a child that not only shaped me then, but would play a significant role in my adult life. They opened doors for me. They made me feel good about myself regardless of what anyone thought or said. They have defined me in many ways and have allowed me to develop and brand myself personally and professionally.

Adventure and curiosity, specifically, would play key roles in the meandering path and journey of my life and careers. They contributed significantly to how I approached and embraced each challenge and change, and would inspire many of the transitions in my life.

YULIANA PEREZ was just 3 years old when she watched as her mother was killed in a drive-by shooting. Her father was serving time in prison for robbery, so Yuliana was moved to foster care for two years before being forced to leave San Diego, California and sent to Havana, Cuba, the birthplace of her parents, to live with her paternal grandmother.

Yuliana blossomed into quite an athlete and by 1999 she was included on the Cuban team that would compete in the world championships. But Cuban officials demanded she give up her U.S. citizenship to compete, and she refused.

She longed to get back to the U.S., but didn't know how to make it happen. It took five months to get help, but finally the Swiss embassy in Cuba arranged for Yuliana to receive a U.S. passport. She traveled back to Tucson, Arizona in 2000.

Within a year, Yuliana was the national junior college champion in the long jump and the triple jump. She became the national champion in the triple jump and in 2004 she competed for the U.S. in the summer Olympics in Athens.

Yuliana overcame long odds to become a champion.

Courtesy of "Girl Power"

Chapter 2

Adolescent Shapers and Turning Points

*I love to see a young girl go out and
grab the world by the lapels.
Life's a bitch. You've got to go out and kick ass.*
—Maya Angelou, author

When we moved to Miami Beach, we lived in an apartment right on the water. My dad bought a boat with one of his new friends, and we would go boating, skiing, and fishing almost every weekend. I was in heaven. The warm weather suited me.

I entered school in the fifth grade at Treasure Island Elementary. My dad took me to school that first day. That day, another *turning point*, would open the door to making my first friends since moving. We picked an empty desk all the way at the back of the room, and when I went to sit down the kid seated in front turned around and said, "That seat's taken!" I was terrified! That kid, Sandy, turned out to be a dear lifelong friend.

It was out on the school playground, however, that I got people's attention. I threw, caught, and ran better than most of the kids, including the boys. They didn't know what to make of me. Amidst lots of teasing and comments, I persevered. I was officially "in." Athletics was my "super power," plus I was cute!

When my dad bought a house in a residential neighborhood, I started to make more friends. Some of the childhood friends from those days are still my friends today. The gift of childhood friendships is like no other that you make in your lifetime.

I can remember my first friends—Judy, Carol, Kenny, Bobby, Vicki, Rose, Sandy, Minna, and Gilbert—kids that lived in the neighborhood, went to my elementary school, and played at the park. This was the beginning of a social life that would blossom in junior high. I was becoming a part of my school and neighborhood community, a *turning point*.

It was around the seventh grade that I began to feminize. I started to groom and dress more "girly." I definitely had my own style and look. I was very petite, with naturally curly hair and big green eyes. I continued to pursue athletics and joined all the teams: volleyball, softball, basketball, track, and swimming. I continued to play guitar and practiced singing (mostly in my bedroom).

My three years in junior high were significant. I grew into my "girlhood" and was included in our annual calendar as Best Athlete and Wittiest. That was a *turning point!*

It always amazes me when people say they hated high school. I really came into my own in high school, and there were *three turning points* that helped me do that.

The first, was the first love of my life, Jeff, who was a year older than me. He was my first real boyfriend. We were crazy about each other. I never felt so much for a guy as I felt for him. We dated for about a year, and although it didn't continue, which devastated me, I will always remember him and how he made me feel. I was awakened as a young woman.

The second was joining choir and performing a solo during our school's holiday program. I sang the solo in "Have Yourself a Merry Little Christmas." To sing onstage for three hundred people was as exciting as it was scary.

The third was being cast as Anita in *West Side Story*, our twelve-grade choir/drama joint performance. This experience was a life-changer for me. The whole process of singing, being on stage, the camaraderie, and the performance just transformed me. I was so smitten with the whole "entertainment, live performance" thing. It brought me deep self-esteem.

High school was a time of discovery, transformation, and the opening of paths for me to pursue my adventurous spirit and curiosity. It was a time in which I consolidated my self-image. I was off and excited about what was ahead!

Tory Johnson
www.toryjohnson.com

Tory Johnson dropped out of Emerson College for a chance to work at ABC News and then NBC News only to be fired unexpectedly a couple of years later. The permanent scar from that experience inspired her to shift from employee to entrepreneur, and in 1999 she founded Women For Hire. Now in its 11th year, the company hosts high caliber diversity career expos across the country. In 2010, she launched Spark & Hustle to produce exclusive retreats and three-day conferences nationwide for current and aspiring small business owners.

What traits would you say best describe you?
Best friend and champion. I'm loyal and tenacious when it comes to helping people make great things happen. I'm curious about people, places, and opportunities. I'm decisive and impatient—I like to make things happen quickly. At the same time I'm complicated—I don't always take the easy route, and I often put my own needs way behind those of others.

What events shaped you and made you who you are today?
Participating on the debate team in high school had a great influence. My debate partner and I became the first girls in Florida to win the state championship in team debate. We routinely competed against boys and it was a surprise for girls to win. That experience gave me a great appreciation for women as the underdog, and also made me realize that girls can do anything.

Who influenced you the most growing up and what did you learn from that person?
No one person. I was—and still am—influenced greatly by the women I know from a distance because I've watched their career trajectory. People like Oprah and Dolly Parton who created business empires, not just fame. I'm also influenced every day by the stories and struggles of women who work incredibly hard against the odds to support and care for their families. I don't know their names, but I know their stories. Diane Sawyer is a larger-than-life hero to me. She was instrumental in some of the best work I've done on "Good Morning America" and I will forever hear her voice in my head saying, "I'm your champion—go do it...."

Tory Johnson continued

You dropped out of college to take a job. Did you ever consider going back?

Nope, never. I realized I loved learning on the job much more than in a classroom or from a text book.

What eventually made you make the shift from employee to entrepreneur?

The scar from being fired. It's permanent and deep. Once I had kids, I realized I never, ever wanted to be in a position again where one person or one company could cut me to the core and strip me of my professional identity and my financial security. The only way to avoid that was to rely only on myself, to be my own boss, to run my own shop, to do my own thing. Since 1999, that's been the most freeing thing for me. It's gigantic pressure, but it's thrilling at the same time.

What would you tell women who are struggling to make a professional shift?

Start where you are. Don't wait for X, Y, or Z to happen before you can do what you want. Start taking action now. And that's really key: ACTION. Instead of thinking and plotting and planning and dreaming, focus on DOING. That's the best you can do to snap out of any funk.

Chapter 3

College and Just Beyond

Life is an adventure, dare it.
—Mother Teresa (1910–1997),
Nobel Peace Prize winner

I actually didn't know if I would do well on the SATs. My grades were good, but not great. I was not academic. I was more hands-on, real, and creative. Math, science, and logic just did not come as easy as languages, writing, music, and sports. Somehow, I performed well enough to be accepted to the University of Florida in Gainesville. I was officially going to become part of The Gator Nation!

Here I was, a Jewish girl from Miami Beach, off to conservative, much colder, northern Florida. I remember feeling scared to be so far away from my family, but my mother, in her excitement, had my bags packed and was in the car ready to drive me up and drop me off. I know she was vicariously living through me.

Gainesville was absolutely transformative. I loved everything about college from the moment I moved into my dorm and toured the campus. This was the ultimate adventure and challenge!

I was completely overwhelmed by having twelve books for the four classes I was taking that first quarter. I'm not sure anyone is quite ready for college, no matter how good their grades are in high school. The first two quarters were the hardest academic adjustment for me. I really had to discipline myself to study. I was not going to flunk out of college! After two average quarters, I settled down and started getting much better grades.

Once I got a handle on that, I decided I was going to join a band. I went to the student center, and on the bulletin board was a flyer advertising a band that needed a singer. I auditioned and Celebration was born, a nine-piece campus band that opened for the city and university's main shows. I was a lead singer.

The experience of being onstage, singing to an audience, and having them return the energy is indescribable! All of my passion and talent exploded. It was the most phenomenal feeling and experience of my life to that point. I was going to school full time, performing on weekends, and living my dream.

I stayed in Gainesville two years, and then had to come home when my father took ill. Before he passed away of pancreatic cancer, I visited him in the hospital many times. He didn't say much, but I knew he was proud of me and that the memory of seeing me onstage many times was special for both of us.

I moved back to Miami Beach to help my mom. I registered to finish college at Florida Atlantic University in Boca Raton. During that time, I lived with my mom,

14

joined another band, and went to school full time. I was performing on weekends and continuing to live this dream.

I graduated college with a degree in English and a teaching certification. I continued to perform on weekends but decided to try the teaching route. I taught junior and senior high school off and on for a year, and although I enjoyed the teaching experience, music was burning in my belly. I decided to go into the music business full time.

I was fortunate to join the Tony Martinez Latin Revue for a six-month trip to every country in Central America. This small show group needed a singer (of course my mom instigated the situation). Before I could say no, my bags were packed, and she literally had dropped me off at the airport to meet five people I didn't know. Again, adventure, curiosity, and my mother's words to try it were all driving me!

Tony Martinez was a cute, older, gay Latino dancer, who had been bringing his show to Central America for years. This tour was more or less his swan song. I was in way over my head on this one. Four dancers, plus him, plus me, and yes I did some tacky dance numbers with him in the tackiest of costumes, all of which he made! Are you getting this picture ... boa collars and silver boots?

For the next six months, we did one month in each country: Panama, Costa Rica, Guatemala, Honduras, and San Salvador. We stayed in the major cities and in the best hotels. I sang three songs a show and did a couple of dance numbers. It is an experience that I will

The
Entertainer

LISTEN & DANCE
TO OUR
DISCO Sounds
featuring
THE DYNAMIC
Shane
IN THE
PALM-AIRE COUNTRY CLUB LOUNGE
From 5:30 *to* 10:30 NITELY EXCEPT TUESDAY

never forget. I got to learn Spanish and live in countries I had never been to (or even knew existed). It was a time of great discovery, excitement, and fun.

After that stint, I returned home and continued as part of a few bands for a year, but then I met a local booking agent who asked if I wanted to have my own band. It was a *turning point*; I was officially an entrepreneur! I formed the Shane Band, hired the musicians, created the shows, scheduled rehearsals, owned the truck and equipment, paid the musicians, negotiated jobs, and had a full-time booking agent. I made fifty thousand dollars a year at twenty-five years old!

Everything about having my own business worked for me. It felt right from the beginning. It was a glorious part of my post-college life. The next four years were something that I will always remember as being the most creative, exciting, productive, happy, and successful of my early career. I was using all of my gifts, talents, and passions, and discovering new ones. I was carving new tracks and traveling new trails on the path of my life.

After nearly four years of working nights and every holiday in bars, nightclubs, and restaurants, I felt burned out. I wanted to stay in the entertainment industry, but I wanted a more normal lifestyle. It took about two years to transition out of full-time live entertainment to what would be the start of my broadcast radio career.

Maritza Parra
www.maritzaparra.com

Author, speaker and trainer, Maritza Parra is passionate about helping others empower themselves and taking their ideas and turning them into products.

The entrepreneur spirit bit you at an early age. Why do you think you had the confidence as a teen to start your own traveling show?
Because I was working with stallions, I think this gave me a lot of confidence and self-awareness at a very young age. You cannot fool horses. They feel fear and they feel confidence. I didn't want to have a regular job that would keep me indoors so I created my own "job" with my horse show. I had worked for a laundry mat for a few weeks one summer and the fear of having to do that again helped motivate me to do whatever it took to never have to do that again.

What traits would you say best describe you?
Resiliency and reinvention. The ability to "MacGyver" my way through most any situation, which means to do whatever it takes to get a task done. I learned this from traveling with the horses. We only ride the stallions in the show, so there are sometimes unexpected situations. During those times, I just had to keep moving everything and everyone forward and look like everything was running smoothly, even when it wasn't.

It sounds like when you set your mind to something, nothing stops you from doing it. Where do you think that comes from?
I think most of the time, moving away from things you don't want is a pretty big motivator and moving towards things you do want is a big source of inspiration. I spend a few moments each day focusing on both, what I want to avoid and what I want to create in my life. I also try to brainstorm problems in different ways to see if there is some way I can solve the problem that I haven't been able to see before.

What's been the highlight of your experiences so far?
Looking back, I think it has to be overcoming those things I thought were so difficult at the time and realizing I am a lot stronger than I give myself credit for! Finding inner courage I didn't even know was there.

Maritza Parra continued

What advice do you have for women who are struggling to discover their passion?
Be sure you go inside of yourself to discover your passion and your path. Many of us look outwards instead of inwards, and we end up living for other people rather than for ourselves ... and that is a terrible way to live! Take some quiet time and "cocoon," which means to close off all the other voices and spend some quiet time in reflection, to find out what it is you really want.

Being onstage and singing to people was a one-of-a-kind experience. This had been my identity. I was Deborah Shane, the "singer." I didn't know myself any other way up until that part of my life. This was a very difficult time for me. I call it my "dark years," because I grieved the end of my full-time entertaining career, but knew it wasn't the end of me. I just had to find the next part of my journey.

During those years, I did many things. I managed a nightclub, served as the promotions director for a chain of skating centers, worked for a nonprofit, managed a dry cleaner, and tended bar.

There were *two turning points* during those years. One was my special relationship with Robert Margolis. We met through music and ended up writing many original songs together and enjoying a special relationship. To this day, we are lifelong friends.

The other was meeting some music-industry people through my booking agent. I ended up doing some recording studio work for about a year in Miami as a backup vocalist. During one of those sessions I met Bobby Caldwell, who was working on his very first CD release.

What came out of that debut CD was the pop standard, "What You Won't Do For Love." We wrote the opening song on that CD, "Special to Me." Bobby's debut album went Double Platinum in the United States and Japan. I co-wrote the lyrics and melody, and sang backup vocals on it. If you want to hear that song, google "Special to Me Bobby Caldwell."

Little did I know that that song, written in 1978 and released in Japan as a hit single in 1980, would continue to yield me royalties in 2009!

The Bands

Chapter 4

Early Career Years

Where one door is shut, another is opened.
—Miguel de Cervantes (1547–1616)

Life is *not* a straight line. My mother's favorite expression to her kids was always "Try it. Do it. You only come this way one time." That expression, and the memory of her saying it to me so many times, fueled my sense of adventure and curiosity. She was absolutely right that learning comes from doing!

During my post-entertainment years, 1978–80, I tried and did many things. Some were awful, and some I enjoyed very much. I now see how everything I did and everything I tried fashioned my personality, skills, and passions into what I am today. The career transition process is about going back and looking at all of those things you have done that helped you to become the person you are. When people are not sure how to reinvent themselves and have trouble seeing all the qualities they have, a visit down memory lane can be very revealing and fruitful.

There I was, stumped about what was next. My older brother Jeff had been in the record business for about twenty years at the time. He made a simple suggestion, which would become my next *shaper and turning point*. He said, "Go to the radio stations and see what they have." At that point, I had a fairly impressive resume of success, so off I went to explore his idea.

As it turns out, I got a job from my very first interview—promotion director for a smooth jazz station in our Miami market. The minute I walked into this small, windowless building and saw the studio and felt the energy of live radio, I was home again. It felt right. I lasted in that position a little over a year and pulled off some awesome station promotions. They paid me one hundred fifty dollars per week, plus gas. About thirty days into it, it was clear that the money was in sales. That was where I was going next, but because I had no experience, it took me about a year to convince someone to give me a sales job. Every time someone said, "You have no experience," it fueled my ambition and perseverance. I knew if someone gave me the chance, I would succeed.

I had been on several interviews for an entry-level radio sales position, but no one was willing to give me a job at a major station with no sales record or experience. That was about to change. Enter Bill Wheatly and WFTL-AM radio. Meeting Bill was probably my biggest *shaper and turning point* during this time. Sometimes you just have to wait until the time and circumstances are right. They were at that moment. On a Sunday afternoon, I saw an ad in the paper for a radio sales position in my area. I called the number and Bill Wheatly answered the phone. He told me the job was filled. I respectfully asked him if I could come in for an interview anyway. He said not at this time. "What happens if that person doesn't work out?" I asked. He apparently liked that question and invited me to come in on Monday morning. He hired me that day and I was off and running on this new path.

Bill became one of my key mentors in business. I can remember driving home from that interview and listening to this AM big band station thinking, "Oh my God, what have I gotten myself into?" I went from singing rock-and-roll to selling big band, Sinatra, and Steve and Edie music on the radio!

The great news was that the station had a 1000-watt signal that reached and serviced a population in the Broward County/Ft. Lauderdale area where lots of "older folk" lived. The station had about sixty-five thousand loyal, active listeners, and we had a blast growing the advertiser base and creating awesome promotions. All my education, entertainment, communication, and community skills flourished and evolved. This opportunity was one of my more significant *shapers and turning points*.

In just sixteen months at my first sales job, I broke the thirty-seven-year sales record for most revenue in a month: Thirty-seven thousand dollars! Considering we sold twenty dollar commercials, I sold one thousand, eight hundred fifty commercials that month. Two years later, I won the Sales and Marketing Executives' Broward County Chapter Distinguished Sales Award presented to me by one of my broadcast radio mentors Bill Wheatley. He also created a new position for me, retail sales manager, and gave me an open ticket to create and generate business in any way I could dream up.

I stayed at WFTL-AM for four years, and then got an opportunity to go to work for a major radio company, Cox Radio, where I went to work for WIOD-AM and 97 AIA FM. The significance of this move laid in the fact that Cox Radio carried three major sports franchises: The Miami Heat and Miami Dolphins, as well as The University of Miami Hurricanes. I got to sell the sports radio packages. Are you seeing this as I saw it ... sports, promotions, sales, community?

I only stayed there about sixteen months, not knowing that a format change was already in motion. In addition, I didn't really like what was going on internally. Since I was one of the newer kids on the block, I didn't have any seniority. What I did have was a sales manager who led by fear and intimidation, and he loved to practice on me. That simply did *not* work for me.

I gave notice and started searching for my next opportunity. In those days, media jobs were plentiful, and since I was establishing good track records, I felt confident I would find a job. And I did, about two months later, at WTMI-FM in Miami, a commercial classical station with a long history and a respectable reputation. Alan Stieglitz hired me on the spot and let me fly. He saw my passion and fire. I was becoming known as a niche radio sales expert.

The next nine years were ripe with opportunities to be as creative and innovative as I wanted. Along the way, I was promoted to regional sales manager. The owners of this classical station also owned three others in Detroit, Philadelphia, and Martha's Vineyard. They swore they would never sell them, but in the late nineties, they sold the group for seventy-five million dollars and then bought back WTMI for twenty million dollars. Alan left, and new management tried to clip my wings. It was time to seek the next opportunity.

That opportunity came from Clear Channel, another major radio company that owned seven stations in the market. The sales manager, who had worked briefly at WTMI, reached out to me. He offered me a job back at the premier news/talk station WIOD-AM, which sold to Clear Channel. Remember, I had niched myself as a "specialty format" sales person: AM, news/talk, classical. I got exactly what I asked for and made the switch quickly!

The next five of the nine years were more magic. Clear Channel was quickly becoming a major national media company. Again, I got promoted to regional sales manager and political specialist. I won the Presidents Club Award four times for our division, and I won numerous other sales contests as well. I had worked my way through and up the local industry and had achieved most everything I had dreamed.

Unfortunately, disruptive internal changes started occurring during my sixth year at Clear Channel. The management, commission structure, and format all took new turns. Throughout the nine years I was there, I had had several managers, and for the most part, they had left me alone to do my thing. But with any corporate environment, it's good until it's not good. Whenever new management comes in, they change things. I started feeling like all my tenure—the four weeks vacation, tops in my industry, high income, access to all the shows, sporting events, and promotions—didn't mean much to them. I could sense the forecast and felt like the winds of change were about to kick up. It was stressful.

As I shared before, for the most part, the management left me alone. However, the last manager (who was hired to "turn around" our two stations) came in and changed just about everything, including my job as I had known it. He did this without ever meeting me, on his way down to Miami in his car on a cell phone.

He told me my job was going to change. I heard him and at the same time something clicked and shifted in my head and heart. I was done; I was sure of that. No one was going to treat me like that after a decade of loyalty and integrity, which he apparently did not value. For the next four or five months, I simply planned my exit strategy. I was going to leave and go out on my terms, and I did.

In July 2006, I gave two-weeks notice to take a job managing two radio stations in southwest Florida. Don't ask how I got there, other than I was ready to make a lifestyle and a career change that would take me to an area where I didn't know anyone. People told me I was crazy, gutsy, and brilliant! I left the organization solely on my terms, with one of the highest commission checks I had ever gotten.

I moved to southwest Florida in August 2006, to work for a small, prominent, family radio company that had five stations. I was going to manage the AM news/talk and the adult contemporary FM. The lesson I learned: don't interview on a Saturday morning (or even on a Friday afternoon) when no one is in the building. You have no exposure to the culture and the people. I assumed I would fit anywhere, with any team, and would be successful wherever I went. I was wrong.

About sixty days into the job, I was driving home and felt very sure this was not a good fit for me. I hadn't changed my entire life and re-rooted myself to feel unexcited and uncommitted. They felt the same way, so we mutually agreed to terminate the relationship.

There I was in southwest Florida with no job and only a few connections. I was stunned and was seeing stars like a prizefighter sitting in the corner between rounds. I never thought it would not work out, and I had no plan B. I had daily conversations with my friends and brothers, who all told me to relax and not to worry. I knew they were right, but I didn't feel great in that moment. My brother Glenn said, "Deborah you have money, so don't get crazy." He had been helping me with my financial plan for years, and had me start an emergency cash account several years ago. That account, plus my severance, was significant enough that if I didn't want to work for a year, I didn't have to, as long as I was prudent with spending. I wasn't ready to do that, but decided to take a few weeks and enjoy the area, the community, and to make some personal friends.

To lay down some roots, I joined a tennis team, bought a Trek road bike, and got connected through my other hobbies and interests. It was fun, and I enjoyed getting to know the area better. The question was, "was I going to stay?" I interviewed both locally and back in Ft. Lauderdale, but nothing was happening.

After Thanksgiving, I was sitting out on my lanai, overlooking the lake, and I kept thinking, "What do I really want to do?" I'd left southeast Florida to change my life and the path of my journey, so I didn't really want to go back to the things I had done, and I didn't want to compromise or settle just to have a job. If I was going to make another commitment, it had to be something that resonated with me.

What I wanted to do was use all of my gifts, skills, talents, and fascinations, and apply them to my areas of expertise: sales, marketing and branding, event coordination and promotion, arts, music, entertainment, teaching, training, and mentoring. These were the things that had shaped my life and developed me as a person and a professional. I wanted to use and experience them on my terms. I just had to figure out how.

I had put together a business idea about six years prior. The idea arose after one of my adult-education students came by to thank me saying, "I'm going to tell people to 'Train with Shane.'" Boing ... I thought that was awesome, wrote it down, and made that the focus of my business plan. I was going to leave radio and go off on my own, but because I then got promoted, I filed the project. It wasn't the right time then, but maybe now was. I had the transitional situation, some money to invest, and the times were changing with regard to business education and professional development.

On February 4, 2007, Train with Shane launched in southwest Florida. The concept and the model were to deliver education, training, and motivation through seminars, speaking engagements, corporate sessions, and one-on-one training and consulting. I invested in a branding package and a website, joined two chambers of commerce, and a professional organization. I was an entrepreneur again. I felt like I was home.

Now, as I look back at the model, plan, and concept I started with and how it has changed, evolved, and grown to accommodate the times and reality, I can see how important it is to be moving and changing with change. How I started a business in one of the worst economic cycles in my lifetime, in one of the top foreclosure markets in the country, and continued to grow is amazing to me, but it is possible.

Here are some of the key things I did to accelerate the process of my success:

- I got involved in the community.
- I joined chambers of commerce, professional organizations, and networking groups.
- I volunteered and offered my services pro bono.
- I asked what people needed and wanted from me and for themselves.
- I formed strategic alliances, and partnered and collaborated with others.
- I focused on my personal brand and niche.
- I gave, shared, connected, and things happened!

The rest of this book chronicles and outlines the career transition process that I believe can work for anybody. The simple and powerful lessons I have learned (plus examples of other women who have triumphed and emerged out of challenge), are inspirational. They confirm anything is possible if you believe it is and work hard.

Successful career transition *is a process*. You can't romanticize it, especially in today's business landscape.

I wanted a new path, a new challenge, a new part of my life's journey, and I wouldn't change anything about how I have made it a wondrous reality in my life.

To find your new path and create a great new reality for your life, I'll be referring to the following four keys to transitioning:

- Everything you need is already inside of you.
- Transition is another beginning and a new adventure.
- Adapt and apply who you already are and what you do best to your now.
- What it looks like is what it looks like today.

Are you ready to career transition and make the shift?

Part Two–Without the Lessons, What Would Be the Point?

I love the man that can smile in trouble, that can gather strength from distress and grow brave by reflection.
—Thomas Paine (1737–1809)

Now that I've shared my story and given you some insight into how I have developed and used my skills, we need to discover your story.

This is where the real work begins.

Throughout this book, and especially these next few chapters, you will need to have a notebook, a journal, a pad ... anything that is comfortable and works for you. As we go through the exercises, I will ask you to write and document your answers in it.

I will refer to it as your CAB (Career Action Book).

This will be a very important way to uncover the information, to see the patterns, and to give you the ammunition you will need to make the shift.

Career Action Book

a companion journal

I've created a special companion journal, made specifically for readers of this book. Simply visit www.trainwithshane.com and download your FREE comprehensive Career Action Book. In it, you'll find all of the exercises from this book with plenty of room for you to write in your answers.

This companion CAB makes it easy to refer back to during your career transition process for inspiration and motivation. Download your free copy now.

Chapter 5

It's Never Too Early
or Too Late to Transition

*You have to trust in something: Your gut, destiny, life,
karma, whatever. This approach has never let me
down, and it has made all the difference in my life.*
—Steve Jobs, CEO Apple

Someone asked me recently if I have always lived
my passion. I answered a resounding yes! It did
get me thinking, though, back to the many paths
and lifecycles I have lived that have gotten me to this
place.

As I shared in Part One, I have always followed my
passions and dreams, and for the most part they have
led me to the right destination. During my life and career
transitions, I never considered whether I was too old, too
young, is it the wrong time, decade, or year. I just kept
moving in the direction that my passions led me.

Remember, it's your new beginning, your new
adventure.

Your mindset regarding this new beginning is
really important. If you think you can't transition and
change, you won't. If you work out your vision, and

plan and can communicate that vision, then anything is possible.

Open your Career Action Book (CAB) and answer the following questions:

- What is your vision?
- What do you want to do?
- Who do you want to be?
- How do you want to live?

Change and transition with no vision or plan is not going to succeed. You have to know at least the why, even if the where is not yet clear.

When I started my career transition process in 2005, it was to answer this unexpected question that kept resonating in my head: "Why am I not 100 percent invested in my work anymore?" The last nine years of my broadcast radio career were just not the same as the prior fourteen. I started to think about what else was out there for a person like me with the experiences, skills, and wisdom that I had. I spent almost a year exploring the answers and options.

This I knew: the corporate environment I was in was *not* going to give me more opportunity to grow and develop. I was *not* using all my assets, and I wanted to do more and make more of a difference without asking permission from people who frankly didn't care.

So I knew my why *and* I actually had a vision, which was to help people grow and develop to be the best at what they do. That is, and has always been, a driving force for me. I took this truth and used it as my foundation.

It's time to write in your CAB again.

How would you answer these questions?

- What is your truth?
- What is the essence of your internal DNA persona?
- What makes you inspired and happy to leap out of bed each day?

Sarah Owen

www.ccmileecounty.com

After working for public and private companies in investor relations, public relations, and corporate communications, Sarah Owen left to spend more time with her family. She always thought she'd return to corporate America, but when her oldest child was in high school she started doing community service and realized she could use the skills she learned in the corporate world to serve those less fortunate. Years later, she created Community Cooperative Ministries, an agency that provides food to the homeless, nearly homeless, homebound, and elderly.

What gave you the idea to create Community Cooperative Ministries (CCMI)?

I have the great honor of working for a non-profit organization that has been in existence since 1984. After I joined the agency in 2005, I was asked to lead the organization through a ground-breaking merger in an effort to create an umbrella organization that would pool resources to provide more effective services. From that simple concept, my team has created an innovative, re-imagined approach to social service delivery in our community.

You've compared yourself to the Energizer Bunny. What is it that drives you?

Actually I had never thought of myself as the Energizer Bunny until I was nominated for the Energizer Keep Going Hall of Fame! The Energizer Bunny just keeps going and going and our whole team at CCMI has that attitude. We will keep going and going to feed the hungry, house the homeless, and find sustainable solutions for those in need in our community.

Sarah Owen continued

What gave you the confidence to try to make this organization a reality?

I joined CCMI as a result of a tragic death in the former Executive Leadership Team. I literally had to arrive at the soup kitchen in the middle of the night and I have never left. This type of entrance did not allow for a great deal of early strategic thinking. Once the agency was stabilized, I spent time just observing the way our organization and the community were providing services to those in need. After being on site at the agency for just a few weeks, I could clearly see that we were providing vital basic needs to people in need, but their lives were not changing for the better in a sustainable way. I began to imagine solutions that would create sustainability, hope, and dignity in the lives of the people we were serving. The reality of those solutions is still evolving.

Fear so often holds us back. What advice do you have for working past that fear?

My personal motto is "fearless." I believe in living a bold life and taking risks but with that you have to resign yourself to the fact that some of your ideas will fail. If you are afraid to fail or face roadblocks, you will never be free.

What advice do you have for women who are struggling to discover their passion?

Stop struggling. Sometimes we think we have to be actively seeking our "passion" to find it. I was not passionate about a number of the positions I held along the way, but they prepared me for the work I am doing now. If you are always thinking about the destination, you are at risk of missing the journey. My faith has played a significant role in my view on my passion. I believe that God has a purpose for my life and that He has equipped me to fulfill this purpose. He wants me to trust Him and enjoy the ride!

Chapter 6
Don't Be Afraid of Change

Courage is fear that's said its prayers.
—Dorothy Bernard, author

Fear is such a powerful and debilitating mental condition. I know that fear has kept me from doing many things.

The unbelievable truth about fear is that it usually is *not* grounded in reality. Read any psychology 101 book, and it will tell you we build up most fears in our minds and make them into mountains. Our fears develop from our experiences, traumas, and situations, which are usually unresolved over many cycles and parts of our lives.

When I was in my twenties and thirties, I had a fear of my mother dying, so I decided to spend less time with her so I wouldn't have to face those feelings. She was diagnosed with breast cancer, had to have chemotherapy and radiation, and ended up being a fourteen-year survivor! That moment, when I realized cancer did not have to be fatal, showed me how fear was keeping me from enjoying her *now*.

This is just one example of how fear robs us of living and experiencing life to its fullest. I have always been adventuresome and curious, and while I thrived on challenge and accomplishment, fear has held me back several times over my life when opportunity has knocked on my door. Thoughts like "I can't," "what will happen if I fail," and "what will they think of me" pervade our thinking all the time.

To deal with fear realistically, I had to figure out whether a fear was what I call GIR (Grounded In Reality) or a NGIR (Not Grounded In Reality). This took years. I still have moments of paralysis, but they do not last very long. I focus on my capabilities, on the now, and on taking action.

Take out your CAB. Remember, this is your Career Action Book and a free copy waits just for you at www.trainwithshane.com.

First, list the key fears you have now in two columns: Grounded In Reality or Not Grounded In Reality. Then, answer these questions with regard to each fear:

- Why do I have this fear?
- What's the worst that can happen?
- Who can I reach out to for encouragement and support?
- Do I need some professional help?

Nancy Smith
www.linkedin.com/pub/nancy-smith/3/b49/a70

After spending more than 18 years as an entrepreneur in the construction and real estate industries in New York State, Nancy returned to college at the same time her children entered college and changed career paths. She graduated Magna Cum Laude from the State University of New York in 1992 with a B.A. in Interdisciplinary Studies. In 2003, she earned her master's degree in Career and Technical Education from the University of South Florida. Today, she serves as the Program, Operations and Finance Coordinator for two Tech Centers in the Lee County School District of Florida. She also is the Coordinator for Business and Industry Services for the district.

What inspired you to change career paths all those years ago?
Every woman has a life-defining moment. Mine came in 1989. I was 39 years old, with two high school age boys and a little 4-year-old girl, married to the love of my life for 19 years. For most of my adult life, I focused on my husband's and children's success. When the economy in the greater New York area spiraled downward, our business came to a halting stop. We had no cash reserves to keep us afloat. Bankruptcy loomed ahead. My husband turned to alcohol and I turned to depression and suicide. Suicide? When had I become a victim? Thankfully, an inner voice told me to get help. I called a suicide hotline. A wonderful counselor had me write a short biography of my life, including what I had not accomplished and was disappointed in myself for not achieving. At the top of my list was that I had not finished college. She gave me one week to figure out how to get into college. That was the fall of 1989. By 1990, I was in college.

How did it feel going back to college?
It was scary at first. I craved intellectual challenge, so I changed majors a few times before I got the right mix.

Did you ever doubt that you would achieve your bachelor's degree?
Halfway through the program, my husband was hospitalized and there was NO money coming into the household. I seriously considered dropping out just to put food on the table, but I was on a path to finish. I got a summer job and the boys,

---

Nancy Smith continued

home for the summer, also had jobs. Somehow we got by and everyone returned to college in the fall.

What do you enjoy about your job today?
I counsel people with little or no hope left. Many times they are middle aged with no job prospects for the first time in their life. They are down and out. A counselor helped me find my way back once, over 20 years ago, and now it is my chance to give back.

Any words of advice/encouragement for women considering going back to school?
Age is not a valid reason to not go back to school. Statistics indicate that older, returning students do very well in post secondary education. In fact, in many ways, your years of life experience will serve you very well in the classroom. You will want to do well for YOU, not anyone else. This is incredibly empowering. You will not be able to do everything. Let others pick up the slack. If you are a woman approaching 40 years of age, I guarantee you have already done more than your share for others.

Don't allow fear to hold you back from living your life. You will miss out on way too many opportunities to do things and meet people who will impact and shape your life forever. Remember: Life is a meandering stream.

I decided voluntarily to change my life and lifestyle in 2006, after living and working in the same place for several decades. I was over fifty, and I moved to take a career opportunity in a place where I didn't know anyone. My friends and colleagues told me I was out of my mind and absolutely crazy, but they also told me how "gutsy" I was. I knew life as I had known it was going to change anyway and that it was time for a new chapter and adventure. I took the leap and have never looked back.

Don't let fear rule your life. Build and use a support team to talk it out and work it out. Get some professional help. Take small steps and do a few things that can make a big difference. Work on the fears that are holding you back now.

I guarantee that when you get to the other side and you look back at the mountain you made out of the molehill, you will be proud of yourself!

Chapter 7

Believe in Who You Are and the Value of What You Do

Confidence is contagious.
—Vince Lombardi, legendary football coach

Why do we devalue ourselves so much? I find that most people do not value who they are, what they have done, and how their actions have impacted others.

Every person has an ongoing story. Stories have characters, a plot, a setting, scenes, conflict, and resolution. In this context, we live out many stories in our lives. Every story is rich with experiences, lessons, and wisdom. We are truly the sum total of all the stories we have lived out and have yet to live.

I have used many of my "story-line themes" during my life and career transitions. As shared in Part One, I have applied the experience, wisdom, and passions I have gained toward succeeding on this current career path. My communication, networking, leadership, organizational, sales, marketing, branding, collaborating, and partnering skills, as well as volunteering and reaching out to my community, have all contributed to how I navigate my phases.

I have always believed that if "you take you with you" you will be okay. Trust your instincts, listen to them, and develop them. There were many things put in my path—by design— to help me know which way to go. Believing in who you are and what you do is the only way others will believe in you, too.

I love the idea of belief in oneself because of how forceful it is. This kind of self-esteem is magnetic. It will bring others to you that are like-minded and spirited. Self-esteem and self-respect are things we earn through our actions. I live with a strong code of ethics and high standards when it comes to how I treat others and serve them. I believe kindness is one of the most powerful principles.

Clear away the negative self-talk and really look at yourself through the eyes of how your support system and networks see you.

When building your personal brand, it is often helpful to ask a few people what they like best about you. Sometimes allowing others to be your mirror can help you see things in yourself that you may not see or believe in yet.

Get out your CAB and let's write.

Queen Rania of Jordan is magnetic and not just because of her title. She believes, "You deserve the chance to make the most of this brief glimpse we call existence. To be all you can be. To help those dear to you." This belief and her tireless efforts endear people all around the globe to her.

- What are your top three assets?
- In what three experiences have you seen these assets in action?
- What are you most proud of?
- Who has touched you and impacted you the most in your life and why?
- Who do you admire and want to emulate?

See the good, value yourself, and celebrate it with others. You are worth it!

Chapter 8

Set Yourself Up to Be Successful by Doing Whatever It Takes

When you get to the end of your rope,
you tie a knot and hang on.
—Franklin Delano Roosevelt

When I think about how people describe me, more often than not, the word "perseverance" tops the list. I have instinctively known that in life when you want something, you have to work *at* it and *for* it. Even as a young person, I set my sights on what I thought was the bull's-eye and kept shooting for it.

Over time, I have learned many lessons and gained much wisdom about how to stick to things, and, more importantly, how and what I needed to do to set myself up for what I like to call the "long race."

Long-distance runners train differently from sprinters. They focus on endurance and pace. In life and business, we need to train as long-distance runners, not sprinters. Our lives play out much better when we prepare for a marathon.

I like the metaphor of perseverance being a strengthening of one's abilities to finish the race by developing a pace-driven process. To truly perform our best, we must prepare for success like we're running a marathon. The training plan of all long-distance runners includes coaching, technique, practice, and endurance. Long-distance runners all train for the second half of the race. As business people who want to be around for a long time, we too must develop a resilience that strengthens our ability to persevere beyond the first half of our marathon.

Here are some fundamentals that may help you manage the challenging parts of your journey.

Passion

When you truly love what you do and have a sincere desire to serve, it is the most powerful "sales" tool you can have. Passion is contagious and infectious. Be authentic and don't force your brand; serve it. As I have mentioned repeatedly, I have always lived in my passion. I have taken jobs to pay my bills, but ultimately I have dedicated myself to my work because I care about what I am doing for myself and others.

> Coco Chanel was passionate about fashion and, as a result, was instrumental in defining feminine style and dress during the 20th Century. Her ideas were revolutionary.

Perspective

Keep things in perspective—stay focused on your goals and seek out alternative sources for news and information. There are so many resources for "the solution" and examples of people and businesses finding and making positive opportunities in challenging times. But there are also way too many news sources filling up the airwaves with not only negative news stories, but the "inside" story behind the story. In turn, we get exposed to a lot of negative messages. Surround yourself with positive, proactive, encouraging people and activities. Prune and shed anything and anyone that does not contribute to your growth.

Pertinence

Nothing is more important than relevance. Know the trends in your industry as they relate to business, consumer behavior, and marketing. These days, *trends drive everything*. Keeping up with the rapidly changing business landscape and technologies can mean the difference between extinction and rebirth. Invest in conferences, training, purposeful networking, professional affiliations, and some business- and life-coaching. Now more than ever it is important to have a

> When Brenda Barnes left PepsiCo in 1998 to spend more time with her family, people questioned her decision. But, at 51, when Brenda became chief executive at Sara Lee she proved that women can regain corporate power when and if they choose.

support system that can help you *not* go it alone. Keep yourself on top of your personal growth, your industry, and the market(s) you live and work in.

Prediction

Do you have a *vision* for where you are heading? What is the roadmap for your success? Many of us at the moment are navigating unchartered waters. I do know that having both a short-term and a long-term vision for navigating any conditions includes all of the fundamentals mentioned above. Being able to see your *big* picture is important. The *big* picture is made up of many parts that have to fit for you and be working together to get the results you want.

Define your vision, create your plan, practice flawless execution!
Get out your CAB and answer these questions:

- Am I relevant?
- What skills do I need to upgrade?
- Do I know my customers, my market, and my competition?
- What is the best marketing and networking plan for me?
- What is my sales strategy and do I have a strong pitch?
- Do I start each year with a plan?

Now, think about your SMART goals. In case you are not familiar with the acronym, SMART stands for Specific, Measurable, Attainable, Realistic, and Timely.

- Write three personal goals.
- Write three professional goals.

- Write three networking goals.
- Write three sales goals.

Write down your *big* picture vision for what you need to do to be successful, and make sure all the pieces are in place. If you are not sure about how to do this, seek out business counseling and mentors to help you. Invest in yourself and your business.

ANN FUDGE is one of the top leaders in today's business world. Fudge made history in 2003 when she became the first African-American female to be named CEO of a major company. She was appointed chairwoman and chief executive officer of Young & Rubicam, Inc., a major division of a global advertising agency, the WPP Group.

Fudge's achievement is all the more impressive because of what she had to overcome. As a teenager, she witnessed the urban riots in the wake of Martin Luther King, Jr.'s assassination. Later, while a student at Simmons College, Fudge met Margaret Henning, author of "The Managerial Woman," who told Fudge she recognized in her some of the skills crucial to becoming a corporate executive.

After earning her business degree from Simmons and an MBA from Harvard Business School, Fudge was hired by General Mills where she set a goal for herself to become general manager of a brand by age 40.

She quickly moved up the corporate ranks. In 1986, she accepted an offer from Kraft Foods. In 1991, she was promoted to general manager of the brand division, a year ahead of the goal she had set. She was also named executive vice president at Kraft.

She insists there are no hidden formulas to her leadership success. "I lead from a core of integrity, honesty, and respect for the individual. The ability to truly listen to all perspectives is the key to real leadership," she said.

Courtesy of "Girl Power"

Part Three–Your Five Steps
to Successful Career Reinvention

Trust yourself. You know more than you think you do.
—Benjamin Spock (1903–1998),
American author and pediatrician

Changing jobs and careers is nothing new. People have been doing it for a long time. But we've become so used to finding a skill or career that we "fit" with, and then hibernating in it for forty years, that changing or wanting more than one career is quite a daunting idea.

Being laid off, fired, downsized, or squeezed out is just not something that most people prepare for. The current employment and job situation is a testimonial to that. Most of the white-collar, educated, experienced professionals did not see this cycle coming, so they didn't see the need to prepare themselves for change. Isn't that why we buy insurance? Let's call our transition preparation "career insurance." You buy into it because of how important it is to be current, relevant, and indispensible. You prepare yourself to be someone who can hit the ground running and who can impact the workplace immediately.

Today, it's just not enough to have expertise, skills, qualifications, or experience. What will set you apart are the intangibles, those things that come from all the doing, living, and leading you've accomplished. In addition to the tasks you performed on the job, have you also been a problem solver, a change agent, a team builder, a talent developer, a catalyst, an anticipator, a motivator? We all have unique personalities and special qualities that we must discover, use, and leverage in career transition.

As I look back on my work path and process, I can see how my qualities, traits, and skills have enabled me to transition through my careers. It was my current career transition in August 2006 that really made me realize how important this process and the following five steps are in any career transition and life change. What we are seeing now are people who are stuck and don't know how to proceed through the reinvention and rebirth of themselves, especially in their professional lives.

I found myself sitting quietly one afternoon in the late summer of 2006, not working, living in an area where the only person I knew was the one who had interviewed and hired me, stunned that the job I changed my whole life for did *not* work out in only sixty days! It was a shocking reality for me!

I knew who I was and what I could do, but at that point I didn't really want to stay in the industry I had come from. Questions kept flowing through my head, and I knew I had to answer them in order to move on.

The questions were:

- Are you stuck? I was.
- Are you ready to transition? Yep!
- Are you not sure what to do? Yep!
- Do you want to reinvent yourself? Absolutely yes.
- Do you need a transition plan and strategy? Absolutely yes.

For me, transition had always followed a pattern. I focused on my passions, decided what current skills and experience I could tap into, figured out how I could adapt them, created a newer persona, and then put my new self out there! This simple formula is the foundation for the five steps I am going to introduce you to.

Simple? Actually, yes. Easy? Actually, no!

Here's a look back at some of my job and career titles:

- Student
- Teacher
- Entertainer
- Singer
- Marketing and Promotion Director
- Account Executive
- Retail Sales Manager
- Regional Sales Manager
- Political Sales Specialist
- General Sales Manager
- Entrepreneur
- Educator
- Mentor
- Consultant
- Motivator
- Empowerment Advocate
- Author

When I look over my list of jobs, I see so many common threads, including empowerment, mentoring and motivating. These commonalities show me who I am, what I probably like to do, and what I do best.

Get out your CAB and write:

- Your job titles over the past ten years.
- What are the common patterns about you that you see in these jobs?
- What are your key personality traits?

- What are the key skills you see in the common threads?
- What life-wisdom themes do you notice?

Below are five steps I have used for most of my career reinventions and transitions. I didn't invent them. I just put them together in a way that made sense and helped me define, create and launch my current business and life path.

1. Discover your passion, vision, and purpose now.
2. Uncover your key skills, qualities, and life wisdom.
3. Reinvent how you can use and adapt your skills, qualities and intangibles.
4. Rebrand yourself by creating a new version of you.
5. Rebirth through self-promotion and marketing yourself online and in person.

Working through these steps helped me get unstuck, motivated, focused, and re-energized. I invite you to apply them to your current situation, and I promise you will find a direction and a path for yourself!

It's another beginning and a *new* adventure. Ready? Let's get going!

Chapter 9

Step One: Discover your Passion and Purpose NOW

You can't just sit there and wait for people to give you that golden dream; you've got to get out there and get it for yourself.
—Diana Ross

If you ask some people who are sixteen years old what they're passionate about, they'll probably say, "I don't know." That's because they are not really sure what passion means to them yet. But if you ask them what gets them excited, what they jump out of bed for, *that* they know.

If you ask some people who are fifty years old what they are passionate about, put on a pot of coffee and get ready to spend some time!

What is passion? Why is it so important to us? If you google "find your passion," you get about fifty-nine million results. Go to the self-help section of your library or bookstore and you'll see volumes of books on finding your passion. It's a hot topic. Chris and Janet Bray Attwood have even written a book called *The Passion Test* to help people discover their passion.

Passion, enthusiasm, zeal, call them whatever you like, but nothing drives us more than these three feelings.

Are they elusive, fleeting, temporary? Or can they be sustained?

Passion is what we love, what we feel strongly about and believe in, what elicits strong emotions.

The Merriam-Webster Dictionary defines enthusiasm as "a strong excitement of feeling; inspiring zeal or fervor." Zeal is "eagerness and ardent interest *in pursuit of* something."

Add it all up: What do you feel strongly about, have an enthusiasm for, and an interest in pursuing? Put the three together to fire up your motivation!

Motivation is one of those elusive intangibles we all struggle to find and keep alive. No one is motivated all the time. Our passion ebbs and flows with the meandering path of our lives and experiences. My passions have always brought the paths to me.

Here is a list of the passions that have motivated me:

- Athletics
- Music
- Arts
- Creative Writing
- Teaching
- Mentoring
- Leadership
- Entertainment
- Humor
- Connecting people

- Initiating action
- Business challenges

Add to your passion your fascinations. Here are some of mine:

- Human Behavior
- Creativity
- Adventure
- Spirituality
- Faith
- Trends
- Challenge
- Achievement
- The Process
- Laws of Attraction
- Children
- Women
- Politics

What is your dream? Why is living it so important? In his 2007 book, *The Last Lecture*, professor Randy Pausch (terminally ill at the time of the book's writing), explored this topic in a profound way. The lecture, which was intended for his students and his children, was viewed by more than six million people online and was then turned into a book. This phenomenon proves how important this topic is to so many.

The opportunity to combine your work with your passions and fascinations is absolutely possible. I can think of some temporary jobs I took to pay the bills, but most of them added value to my resume whether it be customer service, phone skills, sales, or promotions.

Get out your CAB.

Answering the following questions will help you discover things about yourself and help you define your passions and what motivates you.

> Created especially for you, a companion Career Action Book can be downloaded for free when you visit www.trainwithshane.com.

- What are you good at?
- Are you passionate about what you are good at?
- If you could be anything, do anything, regardless of money, what would it be?
- What were some of your favorite jobs?
- What life experiences stand out for you that made you feel excited and why?
- What do you consider a "dream job?"
- What do you love to read?

Discovering and discovery is a soul searching, reflective process. Write, review, see the patterns. Identify the common threads that weave themselves through your life. Test, try, experiment. Take this discovery in small steps or doses, but *do it, do the writing*!

For me, I learned that I have always loved:

- Learning
- Creating things

- Helping people
- Being independent
- Taking calculated risks
- Meeting new people
- Challenges
- Achievement
- Change
- Friendships

Get out your CAB again.

- List your top passions that revealed themselves in this exercise.
- How can they be turned into the motivators for your success and happiness now?

Be open to some unexpected discoveries. It may be in the unexpected that you find your current and truest passions and next career steps.

Chapter 10

Step Two: Uncover your Skills, Qualities, and Intangibles

Be who you are and say what you feel,
because those who mind don't matter
and those who matter don't mind.
—Dr. Seuss (1937-2009)

Everything that I have done in my life translates to my skills, experience, wisdom, and intangibles. All of them count. All of them have contributed to who I am today. From delivering dental work during high school, flipping omelets and tending bar during college, working in a dry cleaners after college, to teaching school, performing on stage, singing in recording studios, and working in broadcast radio ... they all have added to my transferable and personal skills.

The ability to uncover your transferable skills is the most important part of successful career transition. So important, in fact, that I am including these lists from Quintessential Careers (which you can find on their website: http://quintcareers.com) to assist you in discovering yours.

Below are lists of five broad transferable skill areas and the specific job skills appropriate to each. Refer to them for this next exercise.

Communication: The skillful expression, transmission, and interpretation of knowledge and ideas.

- Speaking effectively
- Writing concisely
- Listening attentively
- Expressing ideas
- Facilitating group discussion
- Providing appropriate feedback
- Negotiating
- Perceiving nonverbal messages
- Persuading
- Reporting information
- Describing feelings
- Interviewing
- Editing

Rena Romano
www.renaromano.com

After thriving for more than 18 years doing sales and marketing for the construction industry, Rena was personally impacted by the economic downturn when she was permanently laid off in 2006. She met the challenge head on, beginning a new career as an autobiographical author and, most recently, as a motivational/inspirational speaker and speech coach for women. She has turned her negative experiences, particularly those from her childhood, and turned them into positive opportunities for a brighter future. She even had the great honor to be a guest on "The Oprah Winfrey Show."

What were you thinking when you were laid off?
I thought WOW ... OK what's next? I felt a great sense of loss. A large part of my identity was based around my career; it gave me a sense of purpose and accomplishment. My husband and I both contributed financially to our marriage and the thought of not being able to add that extra income to our household made me feel inadequate.

What inspired you to pursue writing and speaking?
I had made a promise to myself years ago to write my memoir. I am a survivor of child abuse and I declared that I would share my story in hopes that it would inspire other victims to come forward and seek help. With the unemployment rate soaring and with my husband's encouragement, I knew it was time to embark upon my new career and start writing my memoir. I also love speaking and teaching and I am developing classes specifically designed for women.

What has given you the courage to come forward about your childhood abuse?
Oprah Winfrey! Watching her shows encouraged me to seek help, and once I had, I knew if I shared my story, that possibly it would help other victims of sexual child abuse.

What was it like to meet Oprah and share your personal story with the world?
Oprah is my hero, it was a dream come true! I knew that someday, somehow, someway, I would share my story with the world, and to do it on Oprah was a great honor. I was petrified

---

Rena Romano continued

to share my dark story, but Oprah was gracious and kind and she made me feel comfortable.

What would you say to women who are struggling to reach/ recognize their full potential?

What is it that you really want to do? What is your passion? Do you want to go back to school, write a book, or start your own business? Whatever it is, speak it, write it, think it 24/7, and then take action. I talked about writing my memoir and developing my classes for years, and I wrote down my thoughts and goals. Opportunity knocked when I received my pink slip and I took action. My success is still evolving. My success didn't happen overnight, but little by little my goals are getting checked off one by one. Even small steps will keep you moving in the direction of your passion.

Research and planning: The search for specific knowledge and the ability to conceptualize future needs and solutions for meeting those needs.

- Forecasting, predicting
- Creating ideas
- Identifying problems
- Imagining alternatives
- Identifying resources
- Gathering information
- Solving problems
- Setting goals
- Extracting important information
- Defining needs
- Analyzing
- Developing evaluation strategies

Human relations: The use of interpersonal skills for resolving conflict, relating to and helping people.

- Developing rapport
- Being sensitive
- Listening
- Conveying feelings
- Providing support for others
- Motivating
- Sharing credit
- Counseling
- Cooperating
- Delegating with respect
- Representing others
- Perceiving feelings, situations
- Asserting

Organization, management, and leadership: The ability to supervise, direct, and guide individuals and groups in the completion of tasks and fulfillment of goals.

- Initiating new ideas
- Handling details
- Coordinating tasks
- Managing groups
- Delegating responsibility
- Teaching
- Coaching
- Counseling
- Promoting change
- Selling ideas or products
- Decision making with others
- Managing conflict

Work survival: The day-to-day skills that assist in promoting effective production and work satisfaction.

- Implementing decisions
- Cooperating
- Enforcing policies
- Being punctual
- Managing time
- Attending to details
- Meeting goals
- Enlisting help
- Accepting responsibility
- Setting and meeting deadlines
- Organizing
- Making decisions

People don't realize the skills they already have that can be harnessed and leveraged for their success.
Our next CAB exercise:

> Of the five broad skill areas listed above, pick ten specific job skills you are good at.
> How do these job skills translate to real-life experiences? Describe some of them.
> How can what you did translate into something, based on your current passion and purpose, that you want to do?

Here are some of the specific job skills *I* am good at:

- Speaking effectively
- Expressing ideas

- Creating ideas
- Imagining alternatives
- Motivating
- Counseling
- Coordinating tasks
- Teaching
- Selling ideas
- Organizing

Here is how the above skills translated into my real-life experiences:

- Joining a band in college
- Teaching high school
- Young entrepreneur owning my own band
- Salesperson in broadcast radio
- Volunteer for the Humane Society
- Member of chambers of commerce, professional, and networking organizations

Here's how I adapted many of the skills that I mentioned above:

- Launched another business in 2007
- Reinvented myself in a new market where I didn't have roots or know people
- Business education and professional development model for the business
- Speaking, workshops, training events, consulting

I encourage you to check out these websites for careers that match with your newly discovered passion and purpose:

- Job-hunt.org
- Careerealism.com
- Monstercareers.com
- Quintcareers.com
- Theladders.com
- Mediabistro.com
- Careersuccesscommunity.com

Open up your CAB again. I'm going to ask you to make a personal skills checklist.

1. Circle the following work-related characteristics that describe you best from the list below.

Accurate	Realistic
Constructive	Humorous
Adaptable	Spontaneous
Cool-Headed	Imaginative
Adventurous	Versatile
Cooperative	Independent
Alert	Quiet
Courageous	Industrious
Ambitious	Sophisticated
Courteous	Informal
Amiable	Trustworthy
Creative	Innovative
Analytical	Quick-Witted
Curious	Introspective
Articulate	Sociable
Daring	Kind
Assertive	Tolerant
Decisive	Knowledgeable

Attentive

Dedicated

Attractive

Dependable

Broad-Minded

Determined

Businesslike

Disciplined

Calm

Discreet

Capable

Easy-Going

Careful

Efficient

Cautious

Energetic

Charitable

Enterprising

Charming

Enthusiastic

Cheerful

Flexible

Clever

Forceful

Compassionate

Formal

Competent

Frank

Competitive

Friendly

Confident

Generous

Quick

Light-Hearted

Smart

Logical

Thoughtful

Loving

Punctual

Loyal

Sincere

Mature

Thorough

Meticulous

Prudent

Modest

Sensitive

Motivated

Talented

Objective

Progressive

Obliging

Self-Reliant

Open Minded

Tactful

Optimistic

Productive

Original

Self-Confident

Organized

Systematic

Outgoing

Practical

Patient

Conscientious	Responsible
Hard-Working	People Oriented
Conservative	Supportive
Healthy	Perceptive
Considerate	Positive
Helpful	Persevering
Consistent	Honest
Persistent	Pleasant
Steady	Reliable
Stable	

2. Make a list of five situations where you have demonstrated the qualities you have chosen. To help get you started, here are my characteristics and situations:

- Adventurous—Relocating after turning fifty
- Ambitious—Sales achievements
- Capable—Running a business
- Compassionate—Volunteering and mentoring
- Pleasant—Dealing with the public
- Knowledgeable—Writing and blogging
- Sociable—Joining and being active in groups
- Thoughtful—Networking and connecting
- Talented—Sing, play guitar, write songs, articles and books
- Courageous—Transitioned after fifty during a recession

Use these skill information categories to *uncover* your unique and special skills. This will be essential to guide you in your process. It will help you see who you are, what you have done, and what you have learned. It will also give you a good picture of what drives and motivates you.

Chapter 11

Step Three: Reinvent by Adapting and Applying How You Use Your Skills, Qualities and Intangibles

You may have a fresh start any moment you choose, for this thing called "failure" is not the falling down, but the staying down.
—Mary Pickford (1892–1979),
motion picture actress

Throughout this book, I have been fostering the idea that a career transition is a new beginning and a new adventure. Your life as you've known it might be changing, but you still have you. Why allow yourself to stay down when there's really nothing weighing you down that's heavy enough to keep you down? It's a temporary limitation and it will pass! I have found that flowing through these moments and not getting hung up in them for too long allows me to keep doing.

Today, career transition is constant. The days of staying at the same company and in the same job for thirty years are over. You will probably have five careers in your lifetime and for some, maybe more. You will, however, use your unique talents and special qualities in all of these careers and will learn new ones with each experience.

In Seth Godin's book *Linchpin: Are You Indispensable?*, he writes, "Becoming a linchpin is a step-wise process, a path in which you develop attributes that make you indispensible." He goes on to say, "You have brilliance in you, your contribution is valuable, and the art you create is precious." What an amazing idea, that our lives are like a work of art and we are the artists painting it!

The next step is reinventing how you can and will use the skills, qualities, and intangibles we have uncovered so far. For me, the moment I answered the question, "What do you really want to do now?" not "What do you have to do?" was the starting point for the reinvention phase of my transition.

According to *The Merriam-Webster Dictionary*, reinvent means "to remake or redo completely."

What did you stand for at different decades of your life? Do you see how your beliefs evolved and changed through your life experiences? You are *not* done changing; you are continuing. When you embrace and believe the mind-set of the new adventure, it will become exciting, not a chore.

I know that at age twenty-five, I was bursting with adventure, purpose, and passion for music, entertainment, travel, and the arts. I didn't think that much about what the "art of my life" meant, just that it was exhilarating. It revolved around what activities and talents brought me and others the most excitement and pleasure. Period!

I know that at age forty, I was bursting with energy and I had the desire to achieve in business, sales, and broadcast radio. I started thinking about different goals, achievement, and advancement, and what I needed to do to actually get there.

At fifty-five, I made a voluntary decision to leave the industry I was in for over two decades and the market I grew up in since I was eight to navigate a career transition that I am still living years later. I am still bursting with passion, energy, goals, and purpose in a time of great uncertainty and challenge.

I have reinvented myself to become what Seth Godin calls a "linchpin," someone who lives his life as art, and who keeps working on making himself indispensable, by creating and producing interactions that people care deeply about. I have always lived this way. I just didn't know then how to describe it, or what name to put on it.

Seth Godin has reinvented the use of the noun *linchpin* (defined as "a locking pin"). He has adapted this word and applied it to how people become essential and indispensable to the lives of others and the world they live in.

You can reinvent yourself at any age!

Remember the title of Chapter 5: "It's never too early or too late to transition."

Put the fears in their place.

Do the work.

Make the plan.

Plan for your success.

Practice flawless execution.

How do you reinvent yourself? We have worked through two steps in our career transition process: discovering your passion and purpose, and uncovering your skills, qualities, and intangibles. In this reinvention step, we want to take the passion, skills, and qualities and figure out new ways you might be able to use or apply them.

One really powerful exercise is writing your internal job description. This is something everyone carries inside of himself. We don't choose it and we can't change it. It is where your passions, gifts, and fascinations intersect. It's your "DNA personality" merged with the skills you have acquired through your lifetime. It's what you are meant to do.

This exercise comes from a career card game that is offered through Partnerships Make a Difference, a nonprofit organization dedicated to providing educators, parents, and students with the tools and inspiration to do great things. This organization works with primary to high school students to help them realize their current and future potential.

The "Discovering Your Internal Job Description" card game and verb list activity was created by educator Mary Lynne Musgrove, of Musgrove Career Counseling in Ohio. It enables people to identify their gifts and fascinations and to reflect on how they can relate to finding purpose and fulfillment in a variety of career fields and life pursuits. This is an amazing tool for anyone trying to figure this out!

Musgrove says, "It is a myth that we choose our work. People who are deeply satisfied and highly motivated by their careers often feel as though the work chose them." Notice how she describes it as a job description, *not* a job title.

Here's how the game goes ...

First, about twenty cards are distributed, each representing different career descriptions such as:

- doctor
- lawyer
- travel agent
- nurse
- landscape artist
- teacher
- artist
- scientist
- astronaut
- funeral director
- actor
- coach
- network-system analyst
- medical-records technician
- opera singer
- dental hygienist
- veterinary technician
- physical therapist
- pharmaceutical sales
- customer-service assistant

Second, players pretend they have all the necessary talents, skills, and education for each job, and are asked to evaluate each career description on how they *feel* about doing these jobs. Staying in this fantasy frame of mind is essential!

Third, players are asked to make "yes," "no," and "maybe" stacks for these careers.

Fourth, they sort out the "no" stack and write what it is about these jobs they are saying no to. Some examples might be sitting too long, too many numbers, little contact with people, too much lifting, and the like. "Boring," "uninteresting," or "I wouldn't like it," are *not* specific enough.

Fifth, players stack the "yes" cards into sub-stacks and note the commonalities they are saying yes to. Some examples are working outdoors, working with people, and loving to work with numbers.

Sixth, the "maybe" pile is addressed. This is the most interesting and challenging because players have reasons and ideas why they are saying yes to some aspects and no to others. An example might be for a veterinary tech. A player might think, "I love animals but can't stomach the medical procedures."

Finally, the game brings meaning and clarity to what players' internal job description is and what they were born to do. Through this activity, players can get ideas of careers and jobs they may not have thought of before. It opens up exciting possibilities for them to explore.

Get out your CAB and let's write ...

- Describe who you think you are right now in five words.
- Describe who you want to become in five words.

- How can you take your top ten skills and reinvent how you would use them in a job or career?
- Create a job description that would represent meaningful work for you.
- Make a list of ten jobs that match the information you just uncovered about reinventing yourself!

Here are some of my answers to these questions that helped me to know what I wanted to pursue.

Five words that describe me now: motivator, educator, organizer, catalyst, advocate.

Who I want to become: speaker, leader, change agent, expert, entrepreneur.

Job descriptions: author, speaker, facilitator, teacher, trainer.

Chapter 12

Step Four: Rebrand Yourself Into a Fresh, New Version of You

Nobody can go back and start a new beginning,
but anyone can start today and make a new ending.
—Maria Robinson, writer

D iscovering, uncovering, reinventing, and now rebranding yourself is truly an adventure no matter what your age is or what stage of life you're in. For me, it has been a combination of many new discoveries (along with a healthy dose of some fear and doubt). Any time we change things that we have been doing for a long time, that we are comfortable in and familiar with, it's frightening! We are human.

In this stage, it's important to focus on your brand statement and image. The first tool is establishing the who, what, when, why, and how—a great formula to help you get focused. This is the formula most public relations and marketing professionals use when writing a press release. So, in your CAB, let's write a press release for you, as if you are announcing the new version of you!

Here's an example:

Have you met Deborah Shane? Let me introduce you! Deborah has transformed herself from a rockin' singer/songwriter and award-winning radio salesperson into a gusty entrepreneur as the head of her own company, Train with Shane. In this new and exciting venture, Deborah has combined all of her skills and talents—marketing, sales, mentoring, teaching, and more—into a business that guides and motivates others through their career transition.

The next tool is writing your story. Have you ever written your branding pitch as a story? This is a relevant and updated version of the passé elevator speech.

There's always a lot of talk about the elevator pitch—that quick, concise, well-rehearsed speech you have to have on hand at all times so those that you meet will remember you. What can you possibly say that someone hasn't already heard many times?

I recently created a profile/bio about myself stating what I do and who I am. It is my professional way of getting personal and telling my story. Telling your story is a powerful way to engage and pull someone in. Why? Because we all have a story, we all like stories, and we can relate to story elements in our own lives: setting, plot, conflict, characters, point of view, theme, climax, and resolution. Stories help us relate, find commonality, establish a connection. From these come engagement and relationships.

My story opens with, "I transitioned from a very secure, stable life and career in southeast Florida to a new situation and new adventure in southwest Florida in August 2006. I launched Train with Shane in February

2007 after an unexpected series of professional events occurred. It was the right time and right decision to return to being an entrepreneur."

There is a *big* difference in sharing your human condition and experience instead of what you do or sell. Today, why would I care about what you sell if I don't believe you have my best interest at heart?

When you tell your story, people will naturally relate and find commonality with you. The *what* you do for a living and what you sell comes later. Engage others by sharing your personal story about who you are. If I relate, I will naturally ask you about what you do. When you work on connecting, relating, and engaging others by being authentic, the potential for the rest (such as a referral, introduction, and/or sale) becomes possible.

In your CAB, write your story. Consider these questions as you do so:

- How do you describe yourself and what you do in a sentence or paragraph?
- How do you grab someone's attention in fewer than sixty seconds?
- What bold words or ideas can get you noticed online?
- Do you have an identifying byline or slogan?

I wanted to share this story script with you from Chris Brogan, author of the *New York Times* best seller, *Trust Agents*. This is a great blueprint for creating your story line, or script, so that when you meet people, you will have the best chance of being remembered. First, relate. Then, maybe (and with luck!), the sale or referral will come.

Get out your CAB and let's write:

In figuring out your script, let's start with the story of you. Have you done this lately (or ever)? Want an easy way to start?

My name is _____. I was raised in _____ , a place known for _____. When I was growing up, I never quite felt _____. I used to think that I'd grow up to _____ , but that's not how it turned out. Instead, I _____.

Over the last few years, I've felt challenged by _____ . It always seems like people around me _____, but not me. In my world, I find myself _____ instead. Thinking about the next several months, I want to make a change. I want to think more about _____ . I might not want to forget about _____, but I'll try and turn it around and focus on _____ a bit more than the other stuff.

Lastly, when I look back on how things went in six or eight months, I hope I can say that I _____ .

I want one of the most special people in my life, _____ , to say this about me: _____. That's when I'd feel really good about things, no matter what else happens.

You will be asked over and over again, off-line and online, "What do you do?" "Tell me about yourself." Now is a great time to work on this message, your Unique Selling Principle (USP from hereon) and branding statement. By the way, your principle should evolve as you do.

In their book *Brand Yourself,* David Andrusia and Rick Haskins present a simple formula for a branding statement: "Skills + Personality/Passion + Market needs = Branding Statement."

Here are three examples of a branding statement:

- Poised to apply strong leadership, entrepreneurial, and business-development background as a successful MBA student.
- Delivering excellence in operations management, design implementation, and strategic, collaborative problem-solving to the industrial construction industry.
- Poised to contribute strong coordination skills and experience in marketing, sports, and agricultural operations to new career focus in your organization as events/sponsorship coordinator.

Why develop a branding statement? Branding is the combination of your tangible and intangible characteristics that make you unique. Branding is developing that internal and external persona, with the promise and potential delivery of your results to match.

Today, people want to know who you are, how you can add value to their organization, and how authentic you are. Positioning yourself is very important to stand out and claim your spot! My branding statement is "your empowerment advocate."

Get out your CAB:

- Write three one-sentence examples of your branding statement.

Chapter 13

Step Five: Rebirth Yourself Through Self-Promotion and Marketing Online and In Person

Throughout our lifetimes we are born
once and re-born many times.
—Deborah Shane

How exciting to be reborn. It is an emergence from a place that has served its purpose and no longer creates the fire in your heart and belly. Think about people you know who have been reborn. They have triumphed, risen above, and endured periods of their lives that have been dark, challenging, and oftentimes hopeless.

This is your time to rise, emerge, and thrive! As I like to say, "Soar above your current altitude and fly with full wingspan."

That quote came to me in 2006, right before I left my more than twenty-year broadcast radio career. When someone asked me why I was leaving and changing everything, I couldn't articulate it on the spot, but soon after the answer came to me.

I love eagles. They are one of the most majestic, awesome animals on the planet, especially when in full flight. There is a story about eagles that is an allegory but it illustrates the important role change has in our lives. The eagle has the longest lifespan of the bird species, seventy years. Yet, it can only get to the second half of its life if it makes the decision to go through several physical transformations.

In its forties, the eagle's long and flexible talons can no longer grab prey, its beak becomes bent, and its heavy wings stick to its chest, making it hard to fly. Left with only two options, to die or go through a painful one hundred fifty-day transformation, the eagle flies to the top of a mountain and sits on its nest. There it knocks its beak against a rock until it plucks it out. When its new beak grows in, it plucks out its talons. When its new talons grow in, it plucks out its feathers.

After five months, the eagles that have gone through this transformation take their *famous flight of rebirth* and live for another thirty years! This amazing process has always inspired me and has helped me understand why change is so essential.

It is only when we are freed from past burdens, remorse, and old habits, that we can take our flight of freedom and rebirth ourselves in whatever stage of life we are in.

Let's look at how you can rebirth yourself personally and professionally. You can rebirth through marketing, networking, and promoting yourself in person and online.

Are you an eagle? Can you see now how changing, transforming, and reinventing are such important parts of living?

The eagle's one hundred fifty-day transformation is painful. It goes through loss, it becomes fragile and exposed. It instinctually knows, however, that the pain and loss will allow it to live several years longer with all of its physical assets renewed and able to function at the highest level.

Career and life transitions are a natural part of our lifecycle, too. They're only as hard or scary as we want them to be. There are an unprecedented amount of tools and resources available today to help you market and brand yourself to the public-at-large or one-to-one.

In a very short time, the revolution in technology and social media has given us platforms to create, share, and provide information and knowledge on a scale of our choosing. This revolution was inspired by generations that have grown up with a mouse in their hands and cyberspace as their playground.

If you don't think you need to embrace the social media revolution, here are a few facts to consider. In his book, *The Age Curve: How to Profit from the Coming Demographic Storm*, Ken Gronbach expertly documents the changing demographic markets and what they mean for business and marketing. He says:

> There is an army of super-consumers headed right at us. Generation Y (1985–2010) will be 100 million strong and the first 25-year generation in history. Gen Y's appetite for consumption is already 500% greater than Generation Y's parents. Of massive marketing opportunities, Generation Y is the most massive in history.
>
> They will continue to innovate and create more technological gidgets, gadgets, things, and stuff that Baby Boomers (1946–1966) and

some Gen X (1965–1984) will be forever vigilant to have, to embrace, and use. Not to mention Gen Z, being born in a frenzy from the mid-1990s to the mid-2000s.

It has been suggested that the next generation, born from 2010, will be called "Generation Alpha." Generation Alpha will be truly the first millennial generation because they will be the first entirely born into the 21st century.

Why are generational marketing and demographics so important? Because the younger generations have created amazing online tools to communicate and to use to present ourselves online. The new technologies and social media give us more opportunity to reach the masses than ever before.

Making social media connections is a "must do" in today's fast-paced, virtual business world. It's amazing what you can do online, for free, in terms of connecting with your potential and existing customers right now! What's really great is that it doesn't take a lot of time, and it's a great place to promote your uniqueness and your personality.

Let's look at some of the (mostly) *free* online options, tools, and resources we have today to market ourselves.

1. Make Friends and Brand Yourself on Facebook

Unless you have been living under a rock or have no access to any technology, you know of the power of Facebook. Founded in February 2004, Facebook is a social utility that helps people communicate more efficiently with their friends, family, and coworkers.

Anyone can sign up for Facebook and interact with the people he/she knows in a trusted environment.

Visit my Facebook Page at: facebook.com/deborah.shane.

Why use Facebook?

- The user base is huge, meaning many of your customers are already there!
- It's easy to use.
- It has become a favorite destination for people, businesses and organizations to connect and share information.
- It is engaging and fun.

The beauty of it is that Facebook, which is currently the world's highest-ranking social networking site, is free.

Use Facebook to Streamline Your Business Efforts

Facebook is a powerful tool that I use to disseminate timely news relevant to business trends, business skills, insights on social networking and sales, motivation, and more. Anything added to my Facebook page becomes part of the Facebook stream and is instantly available to subscribing fans in real time. This provides a fast and efficient way to communicate with my fans.

Connect with the World

People and businesses from all over the world and the United States have connected to my Facebook profile. I use it as a hybrid, a mix of my personal life and my business.

Engage Your Community

You can post links to surveys on your Facebook page and allow your readers to respond to those surveys. This can provide you with powerful insights into the needs and interests of your readers. Anything posted to your Facebook page can be seen by all subscribers of that page. Can you see how this can spark discussions and connections?

Squeeze Every Ounce of Value from Your Newsletters

By adding links within your newsletters to your Facebook page, you can gain additional exposure and extend the life of your newsletter. This can drive additional traffic to your website, your tutorials, or any other business offerings. All of these outreach efforts can be interconnected through your Facebook page.

2. Google for Business

Assure your business is listed on Google! One of the best ways to do this is with GetListed.org. GetListed.org was launched in January 2009 as a way for small business owners to learn exactly how their businesses were listed online. The site assures that you're listed in some of the most important online business listing platforms, such as:

- Google Maps (via Google Local)
- Yahoo listings
- Bing
- Yelp
- Best of the Web

Plus, GetListed.org will help you claim your listing, assuring that your competition or spammers don't hijack it. As I mentioned above, you'll also want to make sure that your business is listed on Google, and GetListed.org will help with that, too. Once this is complete, ask some of your most passionate customers for a Google review. Simply send them an e-mail and ask them to review your business on Google.

Google reviews (and people saying they found your review helpful) is a very effective way to grow online loyalty, and it's a known fact that it even helps with your Google relevance, meaning it helps your website rank higher in Google search results.

3. Join LinkedIn and Connect

LinkedIn is where professionals meet, network, and connect. It is one of the most prolific, professional networking sites out there today. The potential to connect through all levels and spheres is unlimited. If you demonstrate that you are serious, it can be a very effective platform.

LinkedIn gives you the ability to recommend others and have them recommend you. People really look at the number of recommendations you have as a benchmark for your credibility. It also gives you the ability to join targeted groups, post jobs, apply for jobs, post an event, organize your contacts, send a message to your contacts, and link to your other social media sites.

LinkedIn is being used by many as the landing page for all their social media efforts. Again, join, set it up, and study people. It's *free* and it's very powerful.

If you haven't jumped on the social-media bandwagon yet, LinkedIn is one of the most effective ways to reconnect with existing customers, and introduce yourself to potential customers, as well!

What's really cool is its "introduction" feature, which lets you introduce yourself via a friend or associate. LinkedIn will either work from your address book, or let you search for contacts and add them to your network.

4. Join PRLOG.org and Spread the News

One of the most effective ways to create awareness online is to "spread the news!"

If you, or your company, create news releases, it's really important that you share them online, as well as sending them to your local, regional, and national news publications. I've found that one of the best, free online sites for sharing news is PRLOG.org.

Incidentally, news releases are a great way to target keyword phrases, too. Instead of a typical news title like, "Train with Shane Offers New Service," try using one like "Marketing Consultant Company, Train with Shane, Offers New Service."

Notice how now my title is optimized for the keyword phrase marketing consultant. According to Google, that phrase is searched almost two hundred fifty thousand times per month!

5. Tweet Your Way to Success on Twitter

I love Twitter for many reasons. I have been able to meet many amazing people and have made many actionable connections and relationships on Twitter. Follow me at twitter.com/deborahshane.

On any social media site, including Twitter, learning the etiquette and protocol can be overwhelming. Some people have described social networking as being at a "huge party," where you work the room to make some warm connections. For me, it reminds me of when I was a kid at the park. You have to show up regularly to get to know the other kids, with the hope that they will pick you to play with. You get picked because you're either fun, good at something, or just part of the group.

What makes social networking so interesting is the ability to choose who to friend or follow.

Here are my favorite types of Twitter users:

- The "tweet-heart" who motivates and inspires me.
- The "tweet-osopher" who gets me to think.
- The "tweet-dian" who makes me laugh.
- The real-deal online marketer who cares first and sells me later.
- The re-tweeter who cares about what I am doing.

Twitter is not for everyone, but if you love the impact, brevity, and link sharing, it can be an amazing tool to meet like-minded people. The best advice I can offer is sign on and then study the people you are most interested in to see what they do.

Google, Yahoo, LinkedIn, Twitter, and Facebook all have impressive groups. Spend some time typing in keywords to find groups you might want to join. After joining a few, you will be able to comment, start a discussion, post events and links, and get involved with the other members. Give, share, connect, and watch what happens.

J.T. O'Donnell
www.careerealism.com

Jeanine Tanner O'Donnell is a career strategist and workplace consultant who helps American workers of all ages find greater professional satisfaction.

Prior to being an entrepreneur, what positions did you hold in corporate America?
I did stints in both sales and marketing, but the majority of my corporate career was in training and management within the staffing and HR industries.

What was the turning point that made you realize entrepreneurship was for you?
In 2001, I walked away from corporate life and decided to give myself an 'extreme career makeover.' I went back to the drawing board to determine what kind of job I could create that would let me live life on my own terms. That's when it became clear that I would need to work for myself to make my dreams a reality.

Fear so often holds us back. What advice do you have for working past that fear?
In my case, fear actually drove me to pursue my passion. Prior to becoming an entrepreneur, I didn't like myself and my lifestyle. I couldn't imagine spending the next 20 years doing what I was doing. It was the fear of not changing that pushed me to break the rules and build a career on my own terms, not someone else's.

What would you tell women who are struggling with making a shift in their lives?
As women, we tend to over-analyze our career situation. It's the planner in us that wants to account for every 'what-if.' I think it's good that we research and try not to be careless, but it can put us in analysis-paralysis. Don't put off starting your ideal career path because of timing. Baby steps every day will get you to your goal. Stop thinking that the perfect time is going to come along – it won't happen. Figure out what you want and then commit yourself every week to moving in that direction. Even 2-3 hours/week focused on your career goal is worth it. One thing is sure: It will not happen until you put things in motion!

J.T. O'Donnell continued

Tell us about your Twitter Advice Project. How does it work and how is it helping job seekers?

The Twitter Advice Project is a way for our followers to get advice from top career experts. Followers can e-mail us a question (or tweet it) and then our experts provide information and resources to support them via our @careerealism Twitter feed. We also tweet great articles from our approved experts, as well any valuable information shared with us by our followers. Our Twitter Advice Project is the ultimate career newspaper online, making it an ideal way to stay on top of career development and job search trends. Visit the feed once each day and you will be more career savvy – guaranteed! These days, every job is temporary. So, staying on top of the latest career information is vital if you want to ensure you are always valuable to employers.

---

6. Broadcast Yourself on Blogtalkradio

I think one of the best-kept secrets out there today is blogtalkradio. It is not for everyone, but if you are already doing video and podcasting, this is an amazing tool. This platform gives you the unique opportunity to be an expert and to feature others (particularly those in your community or industry) on your shows. Broadcasting yourself on blogtalkradio is a quick way to build followers, tribes, and friends.

This platform has grown dramatically in a short time. On any given day you can catch an audio show on seventy-five subjects from art and computers and electronics to business, current events, and women.

Here's the formal description according to blogtalkradio.com:

Blogtalkradio allows anyone, anywhere, the ability to host a live, Internet talk radio show, simply by using a telephone and a computer. Blogtalkradio's unique technology and seamless integration with leading social networks such as Facebook, Twitter, and Ning, empowers citizen broadcasters to create and share their original content, their voices, and their opinions in a public worldwide forum.

Today, blogtalkradio is the largest and fastest-growing social radio network on the Internet. A truly democratized medium, blogtalkradio has tens of thousands of hosts and millions of listeners tuning in and joining the conversation each month. Many businesses also utilize the platform as a tool to extend their brands and join the conversation on the social web.

I launched my radio show, The Metropolis, in February 2009 (visit me at blogtalkradio.com/deborahshane). The radio show has evolved into an excellent platform that has opened doors to people and companies I probably could not have met otherwise. I have formatted it to represent the areas I specialize in: business, careers, women, and media.

I know not everyone is comfortable with this format, but the opportunity it provides to share your brand, meet people, and promote others is unparalleled. I have been using this format for two years and it has opened more doors for me than almost any other platform. When you integrate the social tools it provides to tie all your media together, it is a powerful launch pad.

Coming from a media background made this a no-brainer for me, but really anyone can do this.

Here are some tips on how to start and develop your blogtalkradio show:

a. Pick a Niche

Decide what you want to be known for. Refer back to your internal job description and see what you feel confident talking about. Think about people in your sphere that could be featured guests to help you get a few shows under your belt.

b. Develop a Format for the Show

Decide when you want to do your show. Choose a day and time that are convenient for business people to participate. If you're targeting a general audience, then evenings are fine. How long your show will be is also important. You can air for fifteen-minute increments, up to one hundred twenty minutes. I have experimented with different lengths and use them for different types of shows. When I have two or more people on, a longer show usually works best.

c. Develop Your Home Page

Upload a great picture of yourself. I am a big believer in using your photograph as a marketing tool. Write a short description of your show, what the purpose is, and why someone should listen. Add all the links in the "profile" and "show page" sections that are offered.

d. Practice Before you go Live

It's always best to do a fifteen- or thirty-minute test run with someone you know, so you can practice the format, timing, and your knowledge of the dashboard. It's really not hard, but it does take practice. Have some backup material and a plan in case your guests don't call in or are late. Things happen and you need to be prepared for a plan B. I did a few shows before I promoted them and got a flow going. Set up your show guests at least four weeks in advance, so that you can have them posted on the show page.

e. Use All the Media Tools to Promote

Blogtalkradio provides Facebook and Twitter connectivity, as well as a new product/tool called Cinch, which is a phone-audio recording product that can be uploaded as a short MP3 to Twitter and Facebook. You can link your website, blog, and all your social media accounts to pick up your radio shows.

7. E-mail Marketing Builds Loyal Customer and Trust

E-mail marketing is one of the most powerful marketing tools available today. It is easy, affordable, direct, actionable, and highly effective. When you add e-mail to your marketing mix, you spend less time, money, and resources than with traditional marketing vehicles (e.g. direct mail or print advertising). With e-mail marketing, you can communicate more quickly, which means your time-sensitive information is disseminated in minutes, not days or weeks, and you can see the results of your efforts instantly.

E-mail marketing is most effective when it is used to build communications aimed at your existing customer list or permission-based database. If you are not harnessing the power of all the online networking, business card gathering, and in-person meetings with customized e-mail marketing, you are missing a huge opportunity to grow your business and relationships.

Bain and Company provide the following data—compelling support for web, online and e-mail usage:

- A 5-percent increase in retention yields profit increases of 25 to 100 percent.
- Repeat customers spend, on average, 67 percent more than new customers.
- With a response rate five times greater than direct mail and twenty-five times the response rate of banner ads, e-mail marketing is the most effective way to increase sales, drive traffic, and build loyalty.

Baby boomers are avid Internet users. They make up 32.5 percent of the adult population and 36 percent of the adult online population in the United States, according to the Pew Internet & American Life Project. On a typical day, boomers account for one-third of all Internet traffic, Pew found. And according to Burst Media, nearly two-thirds (62.6 percent) of these users spend more than five hours per week online.

Consider too these statistics from EMarketer with regard to online advertising spending through 2012:

- Sixty-one billion dollars in 2010
- Sixty-eight billion dollars in 2011
- Seventy-nine billion dollars in 2012

- Eighty-seven billion dollars in 2013
- Ninety-six billion dollars in 2014

EMarketer also reports that 88 percent of adult Internet users in the United States have personal e-mail accounts and 46 percent have e-mail access at work. So how do online consumers spend their time?

- 87 percent read e-mail
- 70 percent search for information
- 60 percent shop
- 37 percent use instant messaging

We have officially moved to mobile, web, and e-mail centric communications. Mobile technology makes e-mail marketing accessible *all* the time. No matter how much you want to go back to the old way, because it was simpler and easier, you can't! So, point yourself in the direction communications are going, and go. E-mail marketing is powerful and very effective if you do it right!

It is a very savvy person that invests in one of the e-mail marketing services designed to help you create, launch, test, and measure your e-mail marketing.

The power of e-mail marketing is in its permission-based aspect. The database of your e-mail marketing consists of people who have given you permission to e-mail them. That alone gives you a relationship with them.

Spam is a serious recurring concern when dealing with e-mail. In that respect, e-mail is like the Wild West, with no e-mail police patrolling the Internet. The nature of it attracts and encourages people to illicitly collect e-mail addresses they do not have permission to use and send massive numbers of messages. The two answers to this problem are filters and permission. *Please get permission before you add someone to your list!*

The e-mail marketing service I use is ConstantContact. com. It is affordable, easy to use, full of great services, and has wonderful customer service. It has an excellent section on white papers, tutorials, and presentations, and it continues to create additional tools such as surveys, events, and archives. I have had nothing but great results.

Another service I recommend is Aweber.com. This is the top-of-the-line e-mail marketing program for high-volume e-mail marketers. A couple of others include MailChimp.com and IConnect.com.

Now that I have given you some popular and viable online resources, let's look at how you can market yourself *off-line*. Here's a list of some great possibilities:

- Chambers of commerce
- Networking groups
- Professional organizations
- Faith-based communities
- Your city or county
- Volunteering
- Nonprofit organizations
- Continuing education and professional development classes

As prominent businessman, philanthropist, and self-help book author, Clement Stone says,

You are a product of your environment so choose the environment that will best develop you toward your objective. Analyze your life in terms of its environment. Are the things around you helping you toward success—or are they holding you back? Be careful the environment you choose for it will shape you; be careful the friends you choose for you will become like them.

Why is it important to network in person? Consider these reasons:

- It's an economical way to brand yourself.
- Group memberships carry credibility.
- It's a more personal way to make connections.
- It's social and fun.
- You develop and build mutually beneficial relationships.
- Good connections naturally lead to good referrals.
- You forge lifelong friendships.

Choosing quality networks and activities is how it starts. But how do you know which ones to choose? Identify the best cultures to interact with and make the commitment to join no more than two or three at a time. Remember, consistency builds relationships.

The Art of Your Social Skills
Most people are terrified of meeting new people in a networking environment. Go with other business acquaintances or friends until you are more comfortable. You have about seven seconds to make

a good impression. We all assess others in three ways: 55 percent on how the person looks and acts, 38 percent on how the person sounds, and 7 percent on what the person says. So, calm down and be appropriately attired, friendly, conversational, and interested in others. In other words, just be yourself!

Dress and Groom for Success

If you are going to a professional event, dress appropriately, but also celebrate your own style. Wear something that looks really good on you and use a touch of color. Don't forget to accessorize, and don't overdo the scent.

Research Your "Attitude Similarity Points"

The Internet gives you full access to research people, industries, history, current events, and trends. Prepare yourself with topics relevant to the event and don't be afraid to discuss current events, your hobbies, and your passions.

You Can Upgrade Your Status

These days, people are mixing more with others of diverse backgrounds and education. Economic and educational status can still be a boundary, but if you are successful in your own life, that vibe will attract many people to you. Don't be afraid to interact in circles that you might not have before. Build your confidence and have something to say and offer. Don't get hung up on how much money or how many degrees you have. Focus on what you have accomplished and how you have served your community.

Practice, Be Confident, and Be Consistent

The art of chitchat is an acquired skill, but with practice you can get more comfortable and better at it. These days, off-line networking is essential to take relationships to the next level. Commit to certain events, groups, and activities. Get involved. I recommend joining your local chamber of commerce, a professional organization, or a hobby group. Find the right fit and commit. Don't just join. Get involved in committees, become an ambassador, volunteer to help with events. Stepping up into a leadership role accelerates people getting to know you and enhances your image as a doer.

The big question is, how do you know if it's the right group for you. My simple answer is this: If you feel an ease of connection with the people and see tangible referrals or business connections coming out of it, then it's right. I do suggest rotating groups every three to six months so you can open yourself up to new communities.

Test the groups you join. Sometimes the ones you think will yield the best results, oftentimes don't. Others that may not be an obvious fit, sometimes surprise you. Measure what comes from investing your time with them. Are you getting referrals? Are people willing to make connections for you?

There is a great article, "Tips for Making Small Talk with Bigwigs," by John Baldoni, one of his blogs I found on the *Harvard Business Review*, which offers some additional ideas and approaches.

Before You Go, Prepare

Preparation is the key. Establish your introduction that describes who you are and what you do. Have a statement or question ready that "opens" conversations, like "How long have you ...?" or "What do you think of ...?" or "Why do you think ...?"

Prepare your attitude. Be positive, pleasant, interested, and sincere. If you are uncomfortable going alone, go with someone you know the first few times until you meet people.

It is important to balance online and off-line networking. We cannot be effective only online or only off-line today. Each avenue has its purpose and value, but they work best in tandem. We know that being online is smart and essential because that is where people converge, gather, and interact. But off-line is where the true personal connections are made.

If you are connecting with someone online but do not live in proximity to them in person, pick up the phone or Skype with them.

Here are some things you can do to develop warm connections, stand out, and be remembered:

- Share your passion, authenticity, and story. People really connect with your true self and everyone has a story. It's the new "elevator pitch."
- Know your audience. Research websites, blogs, and social media sites, and ask others who may personally know members of your target audience.

- Work the room. Don't monopolize or be monopolized. Engage and encourage mutual conversation and include others.
- Pair up with a mentor or someone who knows the crowd, and rely on him or her to introduce you around. Coming with someone others know and respect says something about you.
- Set goals for what you want to accomplish. Do you want to come out of the experience with warm connections, new friends, or someone you can refer business to?
- Be inclusive and discover how making connections make sense both at the event and after. I have been amazed at how encouraging commonality and synergy can work among complementary businesses.
- How can I help you? Serving is the new selling, and how you can serve someone is the new benchmark for networking. Not what can I sell you, but how can I serve you? When people know you are in your business for the right reasons, the relationship naturally grows. Building trust, by freely sharing knowledge and being who you say you are, takes time. Invest and commit to it with people you feel good about and who demonstrate mutuality with you.
- Follow up promptly and with purpose with those warm connections you made. Lunch, coffee, guest blog, mentor, referral, Skype, phone call, collaboration, and link swap are only a few ways to reach out.

Relationships take time, effort, and commitment. Some grow, some go, but you won't know which until you make the effort to build them. Networking is a natural extension of all our interactions and communications today. We are pretty much networking all the time now, aren't we?

Here's one final thought on spheres of influence and connecting them. Think about the people in all the areas of your life that you interact with. Most of them only interact in the sphere they are in: tennis, church, chamber, and the like. Consider the people who have you as their common denominator that don't know each other, and think about the potential for bringing them together. Tap into all your spheres of influence in your life and make a plan on how you can be a catalyst to introduce them to each other. LinkedIn and Facebook do such an awesome job with this.

KRISTA MEDLOCK never dreamed of being in beauty pageants. She never watched Miss America or hoped to someday be on the competitive stage. Then, at 17, she received a recruitment letter from a local pageant and for the next seven years, pageants were her life.

She competed, she coached and she judged. At 23, Krista retired from pageant competition and decided to create a competition that focused more on inner beauty than outer appearance. Her goal was to construct something that helped girls feel good about themselves from the inside out.

Her personal soul-searching led Krista to create the National Distinguished Women's Depth of Beauty pageant, which encouraged participants to display the talent and personality they felt was unique to them and not try to conform to a mold created by others.

Contestants would be judged on speaking ability and personal style; they would be rewarded for embracing their own unique gifts and abilities.

At the first pageant, Krista hoped that even a few contestants would show up. She was happily surprised when girls from all over her state came to take part in the event. Today, Depth of Beauty has spread to several states and thousands of young women have participated.

"Knowing who you are and feeling peace about it — that's true beauty," Krista said.

Courtesy of "Girl Power"

Get out your CAB.

Don't forget: Download your FREE companion Career Action Book at www.trainwithshane.com.

List ten people right now and think of creative ways to bring them together, like maybe a meet up, a luncheon, coffee, breakfast, a conference call, or a reading club. (We all go to workshops, training sessions, conferences, and events where we have the opportunity to network. The reason that people gather at these events is because of a shared interest in the content being presented. I have made some of the most valuable connections by attending educational events. They allow me to easily approach people because we have the same interests.)

List ten people you have met through educational workshops and reconnect with them. (I call this "netucation," a combination of education and networking.) The opportunity is there for you, but you have to recognize it, seize the moment, and realize that a few great contacts are all it takes to have success!

Can you imagine your business life without e-mail, mobile, LinkedIn, Twitter, or Facebook? No, but they are simply ways to connect people so that they can eventually interact live!

Can you imagine life without talking by phone or meeting in person? No, and that is the goal of networking. The power of personal connections is what "netucation" can and does so well. Now go learn something and make some friends while you are there!

You now have many ways and ideas to choose from to get yourself out there both online and off-line. Get started. Pick a few that feel right and commit.

Get dressed in an outfit that makes you feel awesome, prepare your attitude, be a connector, have fun, and go out there a get discovered!

Part Four-Are You Entrepreneurial?

I dwell in possibility.
—Emily Dickenson (1830–1886),
American poet

All of the great work we have done so far has set you up for what's next. I promise!

Do you dream of starting your own business? Do you imagine what it would be like to be your own boss? Do you have the qualities necessary to run your own company?

Even if you prefer working for someone else, that is perfectly fine, too. Entrepreneurship is *not* for everyone.

Regardless of whether you consider yourself entrepreneurial, in today's world you must have an entrepreneurial mindset. Simply put, it would benefit you to demonstrate leadership, initiative, creativity, and service. You do not have to wait to demonstrate leadership! It is about stepping up, speaking out, and developing your voice, and exercising it for the betterment of others and the world.

Recently the term "social entrepreneur" has gained traction as a result of all the social platforms and how people are using them.

What is a social entrepreneur?

Ashoka.org, one of the leading social entrepreneur organizations founded in 1981 by Bill Drayton, defines it as "men and women with system changing solutions for the world's most urgent social problems."

According to its website, Ashoka is leading a profound transformation in society. In the past three decades, the global-citizen sector, led by social entrepreneurs, has grown exponentially. Just as the business sector experienced a tremendous spurt in productivity over the last century, the citizen sector is experiencing a similar revolution, with the number and sophistication of citizen organizations increasing dramatically.

Rather than leaving societal needs to the government or business sectors, social entrepreneurs find what is not working and solve the problem by changing the system, spreading the solution, and persuading entire societies to take new leaps.

An entrepreneurial mind-set is about taking ownership of and responsibility for who you are and what you do. Let me explain what I mean.

When I worked in corporate America as a sales professional, I always viewed my job and environment as "my business." Without knowing it then, I established a reputation and a niche that branded me. It was based on my consistent delivery of professionalism and good service. It grew and evolved over the years I was in that industry.

Nothing is more important than your reputation. It both precedes you and follows you wherever you are and wherever you go. People want to work with people who are doers and movers, who are authentic and have a proven track record.

I naturally think about ways to do things that connect people and elements, and then I make them happen. If you can dream it and do it, then people will want to be around you and will seek you out! Be a connector and a catalyst and instigate action!

Chapter 14

Launching a Business as a Solution

*I like to tell people that all of our products
and business will go through three phases.
There's vision, patience, and execution.*
—Steve Ballmer,
CEO Microsoft Corporation

In Part One of this book, I shared how the question "What do you really want to do?" kept coming up for me after a voluntary career and lifestyle transition didn't work out. I knew that launching my own business was the solution. It's what I really wanted to do, so I did it! I applied all the business knowledge and skills I had acquired over the years, and then researched and talked to several successful people, and set out to implement my plan.

This can also work for you.

First consider the definition of entrepreneur. According to the *The Merriam-Webster Dictionary*, entrepreneur means "one who organizes, manages, and assumes the risks of a business or enterprise."

If you are considering this route, The Small Business Administration (SBA.gov) is a great resource for determining if you are entrepreneurial. It also explores whether you have the qualities, the plan, and the capital to do it and make it successful.

Whether you start your own business, or own your job working for someone else, let's look at developing an "entrepreneurial mind-set" and how important that is today for business success.

The following information, exercises, and questionnaires are from workshops and materials I have presented and some created for the Florida Women's Business Centers. You can learn more about this national network of over 115 centers at:http://www.sba.gov/content/womens-business-centers.

The following exercise will give you a good read on whether you are cut out to own a business, or what you need to work on if you already do. It will also give you some ways to upgrade your current value as an employee.

Here are some of the fundamental elements for business success:

- You are a qualified entrepreneur.
- You have a potential business opportunity.
- You have a solid and detailed business plan.
- You have sufficient capital.
- You put out the effort to have good luck.

Here are some reasons why a business fails:

- Choosing a business idea that isn't very profitable.
- Inadequate cash reserves.
- Failure to define and target the customer and market.
- Failure to price the product or service correctly.

- Failure to anticipate or react to competition and technology.
- Growing too quickly.
- Failure to rely on others when it is prudent to do so.

Conduct a self-assessment:

- Evaluate your entrepreneurial skills.
- Evaluate your technical and management capabilities.
- Evaluate your business feasibility.
- Evaluate your business idea "bank-ability."

Entrepreneurs' Top Ten
Getting a new venture up and running takes business skills and personality traits that aren't all that common. If you are considering starting your own business, take a moment to ask yourself the following questions:

Do you have organizing ability, personal drive and leadership qualities?
Are you in good physical health, able to endure long hours?
Are you psychologically ready to take some risks?
Are you prepared to wait several months before you make a profit?
Do you have specific expertise in the business you want to start?
Do you know how to find your particular niche in the market and how to identify your customers?

Do you know how to sell enough of what you have, at a price that will return an adequate profit for you?

Can you obtain the money you will need to start and keep the business running without getting into cash flow problems?

Do you like to think ahead and plan for your future, then work to make it happen?

Joyce Bone
www.millionairemom.com

Joyce Bone is a wife, a mom, and a successful entrepreneur who co-founded EarthCare, an environmental company she took from zero to $50 million in 18 months. Upon leaving her company, she started a real estate investment firm. Today, her ventures MillionnaireMoms.com and MillionnaireMomsNetwork.com help other entrepreneurs, particularly moms, succeed.

What traits would you say best describe you?
Persistent. Tenacious. I'm a giver. I like to think I'm funny; I see the lighter of life. Focused and disciplined.

What events shaped you as a child and made you who you are today?
I grew up poor with six kids in my family. I remember not having heat in the house. That lack of money gave me a ton of ambition and drive. I was expected to pay my own way, and I did. When I left for college I had $30 in my pocket and an apple. I didn't even know how I was going to pay for dinner.

Who influenced you the most growing up and what did you learn from that person?
The man I went to work for when I was 19 or 20 was Raymond Cash. He was the first entrepreneur I had ever met. He was wildly successful. He didn't sit me down and mentor me. I learned through osmosis; just by being around him.

Joyce Bone continued

You were a stay-at-home mom who transformed into successful CEO. What inspired you to make the shift?

When I got pregnant with our first child, we talked about me being a stay-at-home mom. We were a two-income family up to that point and all of a sudden we had to live off just my husband's salary. I was in charge of the budget so it was my responsibility to make sure we didn't overspend.

Eighteen months later, I was shopping at Walmart and suddenly I knew that if I purchased a gallon of laundry detergent, we'd be broke. That made me so mad. I thought, 'I'm screwed. I can't even afford detergent.' I was not going to raise my kids the way I was raised, and yet I knew my husband was doing all he could do. It was up to me. In that moment, I made a commitment to make it happen. I did not want to put my child in daycare and I needed flexibility. Having a baby turned me into an entrepreneur.

What advice can you share about balancing your family and professional lives?

Structure your support system. If you don't have a husband to rely on, gather your girlfriends or seek out a babysitting co-op. In the beginning, I paid my sister to babysit.

What would you tell women who are struggling with making a shift in their lives?

Think it through. Do you have the discipline, the resources, and the knowledge? I have no regrets about being an entrepreneur. I was always very greedy. I would just get mad because I knew I needed more money and I knew I deserved it, but I realized nobody was going to pay me what I'm worth except for me.

Self-evaluation test for going into business:

The following is a series of questions designed to help you determine whether you are well suited to start your own business. Each question in this test is a multiple-choice question with three possible answers. Read over each question carefully and then enter your response in the blank provided at the left.

1. Are you a self-starter?

_____ 1. Easy does it. I don't put myself out until I have to.

_____ 2. If someone gets me started, I keep going all right.

_____ 3. I do things on my own. Nobody has to tell me to get going.

2. How do you feel about other people?

_____ 1. Most people irritate me.

_____ 2. I have plenty of friends—I don't need anyone else.

_____ 3. I like people. I can get along with just about anybody.

3. Can you lead others?

_____ 1. I let someone else get things moving. Then I go along if I feel like it.

_____ 2. I can give the orders if someone else tells me what we should do.

_____ 3. I can get most people to go along when I start something.

4. Can you take responsibility?

_____ 1. There's always some eager beaver around wanting to show how smart he is. I say, let him.

_____ 2. I'll take over if I have to, but I'd rather let someone else be responsible.

_____ 3. I like to take charge of things and see them through.

5. Are you a good organizer?

_____ 1. You get all set and then something comes along and presents too many problems. So I just take things as they come.

_____ 2. I do all right unless things get confused. Then I quit.

_____ 3. I like to have a plan before I start. I'm usually the one to get things lined up when the group wants to do something.

6. Are you a committed worker?

_____ 1. I can't see that hard work gets you anywhere.

_____ 2. I'll work hard for a while, but when I've had enough, that's it.

_____ 3. I can keep going as long as I need to. I don't mind working hard for something I want.

7. Can you make decisions?

_____ 1. I don't like to be the one who has to decide things.

_____ 2. I can if I have plenty of time. If I have to make up my mind fast, I think later I should have decided the other way.

_____ 3. I can make up my mind in a hurry if I have to. It usually turns out okay, too.

8. Can people trust what you say?
_____ 1. Why bother if the other fellow doesn't know the difference.
_____ 2. I try to be on the level most of the time, but sometimes I just say what's easiest.
_____ 3. You bet they can. I don't say things I don't mean.

9. Can you see a project through to the end?
_____ 1. If it doesn't go right, I quit. Why beat your brains out?
_____ 2. I usually finish what I start—if it goes well.
_____ 3. If I make up my mind to do something, I don't let anything stop me.

10. How good is your health?
_____ 1. I run out of energy sooner than most of my friends seem to.
_____ 2. I have enough energy for most things I want to do.
_____ 3. I never run down!

If you answered mostly 1s, you are not cut out to be an entrepreneur. If you answered mostly 2s and 3s, but especially 3s, entrepreneurship is for you!

Myths About Entrepreneurship

1. I won't have to report to anyone.

Whomever you do business with becomes your boss. You are accountable to multiple bosses, also known as your clients or customers. Keeping them happy takes good organizational skills and constant communication.

The toughest employee to manage is you. Good habits and discipline are an entrepreneur's friend.

2. I'll be able to do whatever I want and work the hours I want.

Most entrepreneurs do some of what they want ... plus a lot of things they have never done before. You may be the president of your business, but you are also the secretary, accountant, salesperson, and janitor.

Schedule time off on your calendar, otherwise you will find it impossible to take time off when needed. Your time is valuable, use it to your best advantage. Delegate tasks when possible.

3. I will make a lot of money; perhaps even become wealthy.

It takes money to make money! If you don't plan wisely to earn money, you won't. Gross revenue is the total before deducting any business expenses. Net revenue is the amount you have after expenses have been deducted, but before you pay taxes. Pay attention to net revenue, not gross.

It's often a good idea to hire a bookkeeper and/ or a CPA to go over your figures quarterly and explain what they mean.

4. Business will come to me.

Entrepreneurs must generate their own business. This is done through marketing. Whatever your specialty, you'll have to sell, sell, sell. There is no substitute for meeting your prospective clients or customers in person.

When marketing your services, remember that most people will tell you what they need within the first two or three minutes of a conversation. Listen to their needs, and then show them how your product or service can fill their needs.

5. I will no longer have to deal with office politics or red tape.

Every industry comes with its own politics and red tape. You must learn the requirements for yours and establish your own criteria for dealing with them.

Keep current on your industry's political climate and your customers' desires by visiting your local library, and by reading trade and news publications.

6. As a business owner, I will enjoy recognition and security.

You will need to pat yourself on the back continually. It is often lonely being an entrepreneur. The first five years are particularly rigorous due to sporadic income and constant, long work hours. You must have a great deal of personal and emotional stamina to motivate yourself and boost your self-esteem.

Each month, prepare a list of your accomplishments. Look over the lists whenever you feel discouraged.

7. My saving, inheritance, and retirement funds will support my business. When they run out, I'll borrow money.

If not replenished, savings, inheritances, retirement funds, and the like will quickly be depleted. You need to make a profit and pay yourself, otherwise you will end up with nothing. No bank will look at a business with less than a two-year track record of increasing sales plus assets to use as collateral.

Write yourself a regular paycheck of increasing amounts each month on the same day. You may have to hold it until the cash is in the bank, but it will keep you aware that you are not working for free. Get to know your banker. These relationships take time to build. Keep your banker informed of your progress by sending brochures, newsletters, and copies of press you have received.

8. I will hire my friends; I can trust them.

Friends are often the worst employees because it's almost impossible to be objective about their work performance. This makes it difficult for you to manage them and difficult to get rid of them if they are not productive.

If you must hire a friend, follow the same process you would when hiring a stranger. Make sure he is qualified for the job. Have an objective party interview your friend. Write a job description and use employment contracts to eliminate misunderstandings about duties and compensation.

9. I don't need help. I'm a talented person with a proven track record; therefore, I will be successful.

You will need all the help you can get. Surround yourself with the best resources to advise you on business, marketing, legal matters, accounting, and financial planning issues. Good advice is meant to give you a return on your investment. Listen with an open mind and put your ego in your back pocket.

Benefit from continuing education courses at local colleges and universities. Become familiar with small business development centers, small business institutes, the Service Corps of Retired Executives, and other counseling and assistance services through your local small business administration office. Brainstorm with other business owners.

10. Anyone can be an entrepreneur.

Being an entrepreneur is challenging and offers the potential for great personal fulfillment. You have the freedom to choose your own environment and develop the kind of business you want. But be aware that entrepreneurship requires long hours, hard work, and heavy responsibility.

The American dream of being an entrepreneur is not for everyone. If you have the spirit, why not take the risk? Even if you fail, it is better to have made the effort with clear vision, thorough planning, and action, than never to have tried at all.

First Things First—Do You Have These Elements in Place?

1. The Idea

Every business begins with an idea. The challenge is to come up with one that is practical, useful, and marketable.

2. The Need

Make sure the world is waiting for your idea. One of the most difficult tasks for entrepreneurs is being honest with themselves. Doing some hard, realistic market research often uncovers a need, and clues you in on the quantity, the quality, and the price that will work.

3. The Expertise

The more knowledge you have about your new business, the more confident you will be that you'll achieve your goals. If you discover any loopholes or doubts, slow down and take the time to find out more about your project.

4. The Discipline

Look in the mirror and make sure you like what you see. Remember, entrepreneurship means self-management. You are it! The hours will be long, the work demanding, and the income meager at the beginning. You must decide whether you are up to the sacrifices that running a business demands.

5. Family Support

Discuss your plans with your spouse and get his or her approval and cooperation. Talk to your kids as well. Running a business is no nine to five job. You can't do your best if you have to struggle with family resentment.

Start-Up

There's a lot of baggage to take along on your road to success. In business we all make mistakes and sometimes have bad judgment. Now is the time to sort it all out. Identify what those mistakes and questionable judgment calls were, so you don't repeat them, make lists of tasks and things to do, think things through before acting hastily on those lists, and allow enough time to do everything that is essential for you to succeed. Time and money, particularly at start-up, are important to use wisely.

1. Planning

The best-laid plan is a business plan. A business-plan preparer or accountant can write it for you, but you still have to do the thinking and come up with the basic figures. There are two primary reasons for writing a business plan: A) to guide you in developing your business along sound lines and call your attention to any oversights; and B) to provide basic documentation to support requests for a bank loan or other financing. The key to a good business plan is being honest with yourself. Don't fool yourself—because you certainly won't fool a banker.

2. Capital

The simplest way to finance your business is to start with your own money. The next best way is to borrow other people's money, whether from family, friends, shareholders, or a bank. But don't borrow more than you need; remember, it has to be paid back, usually with interest.

3. Partnership

Like marriage, a partnership is something desirable; and, like marriage, it is often difficult. You may want to explore a partnership if you: A) need additional capital you cannot raise through family, friends, or investors; B) need someone to balance your skills or shortcomings; or C) do not want to assume full responsibility and the time it takes to run a business alone. If you go the partnership route (even with a relative or close friend), get a good lawyer.

4. Break-even Point

Determining the break-even point for a service business is more difficult than it is for a business selling goods. Keep a time sheet for a week or so, jotting down everything you do during the day. You'll probably be surprised to discover that only 30 to 50 percent of your time can be ascribed to a specific task or customer. To compensate for the rest of your time, you need to double or triple the amount you want to earn after expenses.

5. Competition

If you have a good product or service, plenty of people will be trying to do it better. Protect yourself by keeping an eye on competitors, even indirect ones.

6. Networking

It is important to be out there today, meeting people in person. Attend events, go to conferences, be a joiner. Online networking is important, but ultimately it helps to meet people where they are.

7. Resources

Some of the best things in life are free. Take advantage of a wealth of knowledge at little or no cost from the small business development centers and small business institutes, all of which offer counseling in every stage of business.

8. Location

If you're planning to start a business outside your home, you may be embarking on the biggest business investment of your life. Before you sign on the dotted line, be sure the location meets your needs. Check zoning, signage, and peripheral expenses, in addition to the lease. Are there "escape" clauses that would assist you in an emergency? What are your neighbors like? What kind of competitive restrictions exist? Is there parking for you and your customers? What is the traffic like where you're planning to work? Who pays for utilities? What is your landlord's reputation? Then get a good lawyer who can read the fine print and triple-check every word.

9. Accounting

A good accounting and record-keeping system set up by a knowledgeable professional is a must. Even the best system, however, serves little purpose if it is above your head or beyond your capacity to maintain. You need to be able to read the figures for yourself. Your accounting system should be able to tell you three things: 1) how much money you have at all times; 2) what bills you need to pay and when; and 3) what taxes are due and when.

10. Marketing

There are many ways of selling your products and services—advertising, sales promotion, packaging, signs, sales training, trade shows, direct mail, and mail order, as well as other merchandising methods. You can also hire professionals to do them; but ultimately, it's up to you to understand these strategies and to monitor them continuously.

11. Credit

From the start, establish a credit policy for your customers, detailing how you'll handle credit cards, partial payments, discounts, layaways, returns, delayed payments, and excuses. How far you will extend credit, and to whom, must be part of a formal policy that should be made clear on your billing invoices and in your dealings with customers and clients.

12. Pricing

How much you charge often determines how long you stay in business. When setting prices, take into consideration all of your anticipated expenses, as well as what the competition charges. A superior image often allows you to charge more than others: customers may be willing to pay extra for convenience, reliability, and great service.

13. Ethics, Environmental Concern, and Quality

More and more educated consumers appreciate businesses that practice ethically, show concern for the environment, and do quality work. It is in your (and every businessperson's) interest to practice these principles. By doing the right thing by your environment, employees, and customers, you will save yourself a lot of problems.

14. The Future

Think beyond today's idea and into the future of your business. Entrepreneurs often suffer from burnout. Plan for the future now, and today's small business may grow to be extremely valuable, and generate enough money to finance tomorrow's big idea.

Chapter 15

Determining the Niches that Define You

The key to longevity is to keep doing what you do better than anyone else. We work real hard at that. It's about getting your message out to the consumer. It's about getting their trust, but also getting them excited, again and again.
—**Ralph Lauren**

The most important things to do when you start a business are defining your business brand and message, your product or service, and your target customer. How will you be a solution? How will you stand out? How will people know about you?

These are some fundamental questions you *must* answer:

- What do you do?
- Who do you serve?
- Why would someone want to do business with you?
- How are you going to let people know about you?
- Who is your competition?
- Is your pricing realistic and competitive?

- Is your product or service marketable and "bank-able?"

Don't romanticize being a business owner. Do your research, especially in the local area where you are going to be doing business. Google your industry keywords: training, flowers, bakery, auto repair, and the like. See what companies appear first and what they are doing. Study their websites, marketing activities, and brand messages.

Most start-ups usually fall short because their leaders don't have a marketing plan and a sales strategy. In the dramatically competitive and challenging business environment, it is not enough to do something well; you must be a good communicator, seller, and marketer. That means knowing how and where to market, and developing a defined, clear sales message. The customer wants to know if you are credible, that you know what you are talking about, and that you can help him.

Marketing, according to *The Merriam-Webster Dictionary* is defined as "the process or technique of promoting, selling, and distributing a product or service." Other sources define it as "the discipline required to understand customers' needs and the benefits they seek."

What is a brand? It is a symbolic representation of what a company is and does.

Understanding the importance of marketing and having a unique, standout brand is an absolute must!

You will need to develop and have a marketing toolbox that includes:

- A logo
- A slogan
- Business cards
- A website
- A unique selling principle (which I discussed above)—why someone should do business with you
- A blog, if others in your industry have one
- Clear and compelling marketing copy and materials
- Mobile 2.0 connectivity
- Social marketing platforms
- Traditional marketing platforms
- Professional affiliations
- Community affiliations
- A one-sentence brand statement
- One word that describes you

Don't underestimate the power of a business card, a professional photo, a simple rack card ... each one contributes to building your professional persona. Think relevant, current, fresh, now, *bold, you!*

Please start your marketing efforts right from the beginning. Take some classes. Invest in some consulting. Get referrals from your network of people whose work you admire. And create your own unique look and style.

One more important thought: *you* are the brand. Remember you are behind all the logos, the slogan, and the marketing copy. You are still at the heart and soul of the company you start.

Think about all the key people who are, or were, their brands: Bill Gates/Microsoft, Steve Jobs/Apple, Mary Kay Ash/Mary Kay, Richard Branson/Virgin, Oprah Winfrey/Harpo, Coco Chanel/Chanel, Malcom Forbes/Forbes.

You get my point. They all are, or were, the face, heart, and soul of their companies. They made sure you knew who they were, what they stood for, and what they wanted you to remember them for! You don't need to be Oprah or Coco. You do need to be *you*, out there being the bridge to your brand.

Maddy Dychtwald
www.maddydychtwald.com

Maddy Dychtwald is a nationally recognized author, public speaker, marketing executive, and entrepreneur. With her husband, Ken, she co-founded Age Wave, the nation's foremost thought-leader on population aging and its profound business, lifestyle, and cultural implications. As a public speaker, she has addressed business, government, and community leaders worldwide. She is the author of "INFLUENCE: How Women's Soaring Economic Power will Transform Our World for the Better," and "Cycles: How We Will Live, Work, and Buy."

What traits would you say best describe you?
I think my best quality is that I'm a very high energy person with a positive "can-do" attitude. Even when I feel daunted by something, I try to break it down into manageable tasks. I'm also not afraid to try new things, even if I don't do well at them initially. And I love collaborating with others, and seek advice and feedback from those who are wiser, more experienced, and/or more of an expert than I might be.

What events shaped you as a child and made you who you are today?
Throughout my childhood, my family moved every three years, forcing me to continually step out of my comfort zone: new places, new people, new situations. I learned how to successfully cope with continuous change. I was also naturally shy but, out of necessity, I developed the skill of being outgoing and friendly. In addition, I learned how to be independent, self-reliant, and to trust myself.

Who influenced you the most growing up?
I had an English teacher in middle school who taught me some simple lessons. First, in order to take advantage of good luck when it comes your way, you need to be prepared to be the best at what you do. She also taught me not to be afraid to dream big. The last thing she taught me was that constructive feedback, especially critical feedback, can be your friend. If you can hear it objectively, you have a real opportunity to improve.

Maddy Dychtwald continued

What would you say is your true passion? What drives you?

My biggest passion is to continually learn, grow, and strive to be the best that I can be at whatever I take on. It's been my mantra and what drives me to both work harder AND smarter. It's also a personal mission of mine to do *well* AND do *good*.

What advice do you have for women who are struggling to discover their passion?

People talk about passion as something that appears out of nowhere. I think passion is something you develop over time. Figuring out what kinds of things you enjoy doing or have a natural talent for is the first step. Then, learn to do those things incredibly well through classes, books, mentors, and practice. Then, find work that allows you to exhibit those skills and talents successfully. Something will appear that will motivate you to develop yourself and your career so that it becomes a joy rather than just work.

Chapter 16

Relevance, Being Current, Trends

Life was meant to be lived. Curiosity must be kept alive.
—Eleanor Roosevelt (1884–1962)

How has age bias in the workplace affected you? According to Ellen Alcorn, contributing writer for Monster.com, "It's the fastest-growing category of complaints received by the Equal Employment Opportunity Commission (EEOC)." In fiscal year 2008, the EEOC received 24,582 age-discrimination claims.

"We have a youth culture in this country, where younger is better than older," says Tom Osborne, senior attorney with the AARP Foundation in Washington, D.C. "It doesn't matter how good you are at your job or how much experience you've acquired over the years. If you're rounding the corner toward fifty, you'd be smart to start looking for signs of age bias."

The Age Discrimination in Employment Act (ADEA) is a federal law that protects individuals forty years of age and older from age discrimination in the workplace. Here are some examples from workplacefairness.org:

- You didn't get hired because the employer wanted a younger-looking person.
- You received a negative evaluation because you weren't "flexible" in taking on new projects.
- You were fired because your boss wanted to keep younger workers who are paid less.
- When company layoffs are announced, most of the people laid off are older.

Okay, so age discrimination is a radical reality of our times, but there are many things you can do to fight it. I urge everyone I speak with to fight back!

"Perception is reality," right? If you act old and appear passé, that's how you will be treated. If you act current and appear relevant and fresh, that's how you will be treated. It's not so much about age. It's more about attitude, persona, language, and culture, and how you stay in tune with and on top of today's world.

When you use the platforms, play in the current social media playgrounds, and speak the current language, no one cares how old you are.

There are four areas in which you can cultivate your relevance, resulting in having others focus more on you and what you bring, rather than how old you are.

Your Persona

Seriously look at your personal and professional image. Invest in a style update and makeover, with regard to your hair, grooming, and clothes. Get some current, professional pictures taken that flatter you. Take the twenty-plus year dates off your resume and marketing materials. Quit talking about what you did thirty years ago! Create a "younger image" by looking, acting, and speaking more currently. Bring your essence out in a fresher way. Build your communication skills and a bold persona. Join Toastmasters, volunteer to speak, teach a workshop, or take an acting class. Look back at the chapter on rebranding yourself and ensure that the new you is someone living in this year.

Your Skills

Make sure you do a serious evaluation of your personal, professional, technological, and social skills! Invest in some classes from your local adult-education programs, or chambers and professional organizations. Check out the Women's Business Center or Small Business Development Centers in your county. Get up-to-date on how people communicate, where they are gathering online and off-line. You may want to reread chapter 11 on adapting and applying your skills.

Your Process

People watch and observe how we do things. In the past three years, I have built my business, social platforms, and my media activities. A friend of mine recently e-mailed me and said: "I'm watching you do good work. Keep it up." That really made me feel good. People watch us triumph. How we operate says a lot about us. How do you operate? Are you in the game or on the sidelines? If you need to revisit the importance of homing in on your dream, refer back to chapter 9.

LAURA HILLENBRAND wrote the 2001 best-selling book "Seabiscuit: An American Legend," the work from which the 2003 feature film "Seabiscuit" was adapted. It was the story of the underdog horse that captivated the nation in 1938.

While writing "Seabiscuit," Hillenbrand suffered through a terrifying 10-year cycle of health problems that made normal life challenging and writing improbable. Her ordeal began in 1987, when she was just 19. Years later, a doctor diagnosed her with CFS, Chronic Fatigue Syndrome.

Experts describe the illness as a complex disorder characterized by debilitating fatigue that is not improved by bed rest and that may be worsened by physical or mental activity. Because of her illness, Hillenbrand dropped out of school and was unable to handle full-time work.

Seabiscuit came along just in time. Her research led her to fall in love with the story of three men beset by hardship who reassembled their lives around the little horse. Writing the story was a momentary escape from her circumstances and she found ways to write despite her illness.

"Seabiscuit" earned numerous honors and won critical acclaim as one of the top books of 2001. More importantly, it gave Hillenbrand the opportunity for a new life.

"When I was writing, I became a storyteller, not an invalid. My life had a purpose to it," she said.

Courtesy of "Girl Power"

Your Platforms

It's *not* negotiable to say "I'm not using any social platform" if you're networking online and/or searching for a job or career. You must have a LinkedIn profile and you must start using your Facebook account more! The benefits of using social platforms are far reaching. Ask a friend or your children to sit down and help you. It's an important investment. You do realize that people are googling you right? If you are not linking yourself to Facebook, LinkedIn, Twitter, or YouTube, you are not going to be considered a player. You don't have to be active on every site, but you do need to be on one or two. For more information on the importance of being connected, turn back to chapter 13.

So, how do your persona, skills, process, and platforms impact your image? They all work together to make you available and accessible, and to broaden your reach. Creating the right image will go far and just may lead to your next big job, sale, break, or lead!

"Leaders are people who can discern the inevitable and act accordingly. When people talk about business acumen, discernment is a big part of it. It's a bit like gut instinct, but a little more developed." Donald Trump

Chapter 17

Empowering Women in Business and Social Leadership

*I learned you have to trust yourself,
be what you are, and do what you
ought to do the way you should do it.*
—Barbra Streisand

Women have the opportunity to make a *big* difference and change things *now!* We are a majority, a coveted demographic, and a powerful economic force.

If you're a woman, I highly recommend you read the following four books:

- *The Age Curve: How to Profit from the Coming Demographic Storm*, by Ken Gronbach.
- *Influence: How Women's Soaring Economic Power Will Transform Our World for the Better*, by Maddy Dychtwald and Christine Larson.
- *Womenomics: Work Less, Achieve More, Live Better*, by Claire Shipman and Katty Kay.
- *Fired to Hired: Bouncing Back from Job Loss to Get to Work Right Now*, by Tory Johnson.

Why are women poised to make a huge difference and to start changing things *now*? Check out these statistics:

- Women make up 52 percent of the work force.
- Women make up 60 percent of college students.
- Women do 66 percent of global spending.
- Women hold 51.3 percent of global wealth.
- Twice as many businesses are started by women than by men.
- Women hold 51 percent of all management/ professional positions in the United States.

So why are we still so reluctant to step up, step out, and exercise more leadership and self-confidence?

I see women's willingness to remain in the shadows as a result, in part, of how women have been socialized. Women are not necessarily encouraged (and in turn, motivated) to step up in business leadership. And yet, women have the opportunity to have any work-life balance that they want, be it married with children, a single parent, single with no kids, or married with no kids. Anything goes and is possible!

In the book *Influence*, authors Dychtwald and Larson document the findings of a U.S. survey performed by financial-services company Allianz and Harris Interactive. For this survey, three thousand random men and women answered questions on gender, money, and power.

The findings?

- Money means security to women, freedom to men.
- Men see themselves as warriors, women as worriers.
- Women put the financial needs of others ahead of their own.

The results indicated that confidence, leadership, and independence are all tied into financial freedom. At this point women have a lot of ground to make up, but the future looks *very* bright.

The authors call women "a sleeping giantess of collective untapped economic power fully awakened." They go on to say, "The speed of the journey is up to women." I couldn't agree more with regard to women taking full responsibility to hone their skills, develop their leadership qualities, and express their voice. Women are fearful to take an active role in business because of their socialization. It is time for them to step out and move on from that old model.

Women can use their feminine energy, emotional intelligence, intuition, and heart to lead. It begins with girls and continues with women of all ages.

What can and should we do?

- Invest in and encourage financial education and professional skills development.
- Support women in business and politics.
- Mentor young women and older women in transition.

- Invest in companies that support equal pay and implement family-friendly work policies.
- Empower men to help build a "we" world.
- Use social platforms to share ideas and information about efforts for women to help themselves.

We can accelerate the shift, and along the way we can learn how to empower ourselves to be ready for leadership, success, and financial independence.

This is *not* a feminist perspective on women and work. The perspective is seeking fundamentals for women—equality and opportunity for women and men to be equal partners and stewards of the future. Women are not arriving; we are here and we've been here. We are simply shifting to our rightful place as 50 percent of the world's citizens who now have a majority of the economic power!

Empower yourself *now*. Take the initiative to change!

Chapter 18

Some Personal Thoughts in Summary

*The soul should always stand ajar. Ready
to welcome the ecstatic experience.*
Emily Dickinson (1830–1886), poet

Writing this book has been an amazing journey for me. It has affirmed for me that everything I need to be successful is right inside of me and right in front of me.

We are born once and reborn many times. Changes and transitions in our lives can be very scary. Starting from a place of not knowing, and moving to understanding and belief (where we see things more clearly), are how we grow and gain wisdom. We must navigate both because both have their purpose and each helps define the other.

This book has been a labor of love, and I hope that I've met my goal of helping and inspiring you to be much more active in whatever career change and transition you are going through.

Make the shift. Your career transition is a new beginning and a new adventure. Make the discovery and journey fun! Believe in yourself. Set yourself up to succeed today. Be open to the unexpected. Follow your heart and lead with your passions. Do the work. Celebrate yourself.

It is my sincere hope that after reading this book and working the exercises you will ... "soar above your current altitude and fly with full wingspan."

Thanks for allowing me to be a part of your journey!

Appendix 1

How To Get Your Free Companion Career Action Book

In each chapter, I've asked a lot of questions and maybe you answered them as you read along. But, in case you didn't, I've compiled them all here in one handy section for you to answer them at your own pace.

Career Action Book

a companion journal

To be used with
Deborah Shane's book:
Career Transition-make the shift
The 5 Steps to Successful Career Reinvention

Or, you can simply visit www.trainwithshane.com and download the free special companion journal which features all of these exercises with plenty of room for you to write your answers.

From Part One: My Story
List five key personal shapers and turning points in your life.

From Chapter 5: It's Never Too Early or Too Late to Transition
1. What is your vision?
2. What do you want to do?
3. Who do you want to be?
4. How do you want to live?
5. What is your truth?
6. What is the essence of your internal DNA persona?
7. What makes you inspired and happy to leap out of bed each day?

From Chapter 6: Don't Be Afraid of Change
First, list the key fears you have *now* in two columns: Grounded In Reality or Not Grounded In Reality. Then, answer these questions with regard to each fear:
1. Why do I have this fear?
2. What's the worst that can happen?
3. Who can I reach out to for encouragement and support?
4. Do I need some professional help?

From Chapter 7: Believe in Who You Are and the Value of What You Do
1. What are your top three assets?
2. In what three experiences have you seen these assets in action?
3. What are you most proud of?
4. Who has touched you and impacted you the most in your life and why?
5. Who do you admire and want to emulate?

From Chapter 8: Set Yourself Up to Be Successful by Doing Whatever It Takes
1   Am I relevant?
2   What skills do I need to upgrade?
3   Do I know my customers, my market, and my competition?
4   What is the best marketing and networking plan for me?
5   What is my sales strategy and do I have a strong pitch?
6   Do I start each year with a plan?

Think about your SMART goals: Specific, Measurable, Attainable, Realistic, and Timely.

1   Write three personal goals.
2   Write three professional goals.
3   Write three networking goals.
4   Write three sales goals.

From Part Three: The Five Steps to Successful Career Transition

1. List your job titles over the past ten years.
2. What are the common threads you see in these jobs?
3. What are your key personality traits?
4. What are the key skills you see in the common threads?
5. What life-wisdom themes do you notice?

From Chapter 9: Discover Your Passion and Purpose Now

1. What are you good at?
2. Are you passionate about what you are good at?
3. If you could be anything, do anything, regardless of money, what would it be?
4. What were some of your favorite jobs?
5. What life experiences stand out for you that made you feel excited, and why?
6. What do you consider a "dream job?"
7. What do you love to read?

List the top passions that revealed themselves in this exercise.
How can they be turned into the motivators for your success and happiness now?

From Chapter 10: Uncover your Skills, Qualities, and Intangibles

Refer to the five broad skill areas (they are listed in Chapter 10). Pick ten specific job skills you are good at.

1. How do these job skills translate to real-life experiences? Describe some of them.

2. How can what you did translate into something, based on your passion and purpose, that you want to do?

Refer to the work-related characteristics list (Chapter 10) and choose those that describe you best.

Make a list of the five situations where you have demonstrated the qualities you have chosen.

From Chapter 11: Reinvent by Adapting and Applying How You Use Your Skills and Qualities

1. Describe who you think you are right now in five words.

2. Describe who you want to become in five words.

3. How can you take your top ten skills and reinvent how you would use them in a job or career

4. Create a job description that would represent meaningful work for you.

5. Make a list of ten jobs that match information you just uncovered about reinventing yourself!

From Chapter 12: Rebrand Yourself and Create a New Version of You

Write a press release for you, as if you are announcing the new version of you!

Here's an example:

Have you met Deborah Shane? Let me introduce you! Deborah has transformed herself from a rockin' singer/songwriter and award-winning radio salesperson into a gusty entrepreneur as the head of her own company, Train with Shane. In this new and exciting venture, Deborah has combined all of her skills and talents—marketing, sales, mentoring, teaching, and more—into a business that guides and motivates others through their career transition.

In figuring out your script, let's start with the story of you. Have you done this lately (or ever)? Want an easy way to start?

My name is _____. I was raised in _____ , a place known for _____. When I was growing up, I never quite felt _____. I used to think that I'd grow up to _____ , but that's not how it turned out. Instead, I _____.

Over the last few years, I've felt challenged by _____ . It always seems like people around me _____, but not me. In my world, I find myself _____ instead.

Thinking about the next several months, I want to make a change. I want to think more about _____ . I might not want to forget about _____, but I'll try and turn it around and focus on _____ a bit more than the other stuff.

Lastly, when I look back on how things went in six or eight months, I hope I can say that I _____ .
I want one of the most special people in my life, _____ , to say this about me: _____. That's when I'd feel really good about things, no matter what else happens.

Consider these questions when developing your story:
1. How do you describe yourself and what you do in a sentence or paragraph?
2. How do you grab someone's attention in fewer than sixty seconds?
3. What bold words or ideas can get you noticed online?
4. Do you have an identifying byline or slogan?
Write three one-sentence examples of your branding statement.

From Chapter 13: Rebirth Yourself Through Self-Promotion and Marketing Online and In Person
List ten people right now and think of creative ways to bring them together, like maybe a meet up, a luncheon, coffee, breakfast, a conference call, or a reading club.
List ten people you have met through educational workshops and reconnect with them. (I call this "netucation," a combination of education and networking.)
From Chapter 14: Launching a Business as a Solution
If you are considering starting your own business, take a moment to ask yourself the following questions:

Do you have organizing ability, personal drive and leadership qualities?
Are you in good physical health,
able to endure long hours?
Are you psychologically ready to take some risks?
Are you prepared to wait several
months before you make a profit?
Do you have specific expertise in
the business you want to start?
Do you know how to find your particular niche in
the market and how to identify your customers?
Do you know how to sell enough of
what you have, at a price that will
return an adequate profit for you?
Can you obtain the money you will need
to start and keep the business running without getting into cash flow problems?
Do you like to think ahead and plan for your
future, then work to make it happen?

Self-evaluation test for going into business:
The following is a series of questions designed to help
you determine whether you are well suited to start your
own business. Each question in this test is a multiple-
choice question with three possible answers. Read over
each question carefully and then enter your response
in the blank provided at the left.

1. Are you a self-starter?
_____ 1. Easy does it. I don't put myself out until I have
to.
_____ 2. If someone gets me started, I keep going all
right.

_____ 3. I do things on my own. Nobody has to tell me to get going.

2. How do you feel about other people?
_____ 1. Most people irritate me.
_____ 2. I have plenty of friends—I don't need anyone else.
_____ 3. I like people. I can get along with just about anybody.

3. Can you lead others?
_____ 1. I let someone else get things moving. Then I go along if I feel like it.
_____ 2. I can give the orders if someone else tells me what we should do.
_____ 3. I can get most people to go along when I start something.

4. Can you take responsibility?
_____ 1. There's always some eager beaver around wanting to show how smart he is. I say, let him.
_____ 2. I'll take over if I have to, but I'd rather let someone else be responsible.
_____ 3. I like to take charge of things and see them through.

5. Are you a good organizer?
_____ 1. You get all set and then something comes along and presents too many problems. So I just take things as they come.
_____ 2. I do all right unless things get confused. Then I quit.

_____ 3. I like to have a plan before I start. I'm usually the one to get things lined up when the group wants to do something.

6. Are you a committed worker?

_____ 1. I can't see that hard work gets you anywhere.

_____ 2. I'll work hard for a while, but when I've had enough, that's it.

_____ 3. I can keep going as long as I need to. I don't mind working hard for something I want.

7. Can you make decisions?

_____ 1. I don't like to be the one who has to decide things.

_____ 2. I can if I have plenty of time. If I have to make up my mind fast, I think later I should have decided the other way.

_____ 3. I can make up my mind in a hurry if I have to. It usually turns out okay, too.

8. Can people trust what you say?

_____ 1. Why bother if the other fellow doesn't know the difference.

_____ 2. I try to be on the level most of the time, but sometimes I just say what's easiest.

_____ 3. You bet they can. I don't say things I don't mean.

9. Can you see a project through to the end?

_____ 1. If it doesn't go right, I quit. Why beat your brains out?

_____ 2. I usually finish what I start—if it goes well.

_____ 3. If I make up my mind to do something, I don't let anything stop me.

10. How good is your health?
_____ 1. I run out of energy sooner than most of my friends seem to.
_____ 2. I have enough energy for most things I want to do.
_____ 3. I never run down!

Appendix 2

Resources

The following are a few of my favorite things, from websites and books to blogs and people in the industry I respect.

<u>Professional Development</u>

Books

The Happiness Project: Or, Why I Spent a Year Trying to Sing in the Morning, Clean My Closets, Fight Right, Read Aristotle, and Generally Have More Fun, by Gretchen Rubin
The Happiness Hypothesis: Finding Modern Truth in Ancient Wisdom, by Jonathan Haidt
The Last Lecture by Randy Pausch
Outliers: The Story of Success by Malcolm Gladwell

Websites and Blogs

Deborahshanetoolbox.com:Deliveringempowerment, motivation, business education, and professional development
TonyRobbins.com: Strategies to improve the quality of your life

PersistenceUnlimited.com: How to set your goals and reach them

StevePavlina.com: A site to guide and inspire you to accept your life's purpose

ThinkSimpleNow.com: A site that empowers people to find inner clarity and personal happiness

PickTheBrain.com: Anything related to self improvement

PluginID.com: A site about helping you realize who you are and who you are not

IlluminatedMind.com: To empower and emancipate your most authentic self

Business and Entrepreneurship

Books

Linchpin: Are You Indispensable? by Seth Godin

Millionaire Moms: The Art of Raising a Business and a Family at the Same Time, By Joyce Bone

Will Work From Home: Earn the Cash—Without the Commute, by Tory Johnson

The Element: How Finding Your Passion Changes Everything, by Ken Robinson

The Age Curve: How to Profit from the Coming Demographic Storm, by Ken Gronbach

Brand Yourself: How to Create an Identity for a Brilliant Career, by David Andrusia and Rick Haskins

Influence: How Women's Soaring Economic Power will Transform Our World for the Better, by Maddy Dychtwald and Christine Larson

Websites and Blogs

Catalyst.org: Expanding opportunities for women and business

Trendwatching.com: Global tracking of consumer, marketing, and business trends

Coolbusinessideas.com: Gathering new promising business ideas and opportunities from around the world

Huffingtonpost.com: The Internet newspaper

Sba.org: Small Business Administration

Smallbiztrends.com: A great site to stay informed about the small business market

Ashoka.org: Working with social entrepreneurs and their innovations to create positive social change

Lifehacker.com: Tips, shortcuts and downloads that help get things done smarter and more efficiently

SmallBusinessBrief.com: A collection of the best small business articles

DuctTapeMarketing.com: Simple, effective and affordable small business marketing

Careers and Jobs

Books

Fired to Hired: Bouncing Back from Job Loss to Get to Work Right Now, by Tory Johnson

Women for Hire's Get-Ahead Guide to Career Success, by Tory Johnson and Robyn Freedman Spizman

Women for Hire: The Ultimate Guide to Getting a Job, by Tory Johnson and Robyn Freedman Spizman

Who Moved My Cheese? by Spencer Johnson and Kenneth Blanchard

It's Not Just Who You Know: Transform Your Life (and Your Organization) by Turning Colleagues and Contacts into Lasting, Genuine Relationships, by Tommy Spaulding and Ken Blancard
What Color is Your Parachute?: A Practical Manual for Jog-Hunters and Career-Changers, by Richard Nelson Bolles

Websites and Blogs

CareerRealism.com: A sharing of thoughts, trends, and ways to say employable long-term

WomenForHire.com: Comprehensive recruitment services for women

QuintCareers.com: A leader in career and job-search advice

Job-hunt.org: Connect to your new job here

FLWBC.org: Florida Women's Business Center is a small business resource dedicated to the individual professional development of women

Careerthoughtleaders.com: Your think tank for the now, the new, and the next

CareerBuilder.com: Matching the right people with the right jobs

Monster.com: Career advice and job search

SecretsoftheJobHunt.com: A social network for job seekers and career advice professionals

AllThingsWorkplace.com: Practical ways to become extraordinary

BrazenCareerist.com: Advice at the intersection of work and life

Social Media and Network Marketing

Books

The Zen of Social Media Marketing: An Easier Way to Build Credibility, Generate Buzz, and Increase Revenue, by Shama Kabani and Chris Brogan

Facebook Marketing: Leverage Social Media to Grow Your Business, by Steven Holzner

Twitterville: How Businesses Can Thrive in the New Global Neighborhoods, by Shel Israel

The Digital Handshake: Seven Proven Strategies to Grow Your Business Using Social Media, by Paul Chaney

Twitter Power 2.0: How to Dominate Your Market One Tweet at a Time, by Joel Comm and Anthony Robbins

Tribes: We Need You to Lead Us, by Seth Godin

Trust Agents by Chris Brogan

Success Secrets of the Social Media Marketing Superstars by Mitch Meyerson

The Complete Idiot's Guide to Social Media Marketing, by Jennifer Abernethy

Websites & Blogs

LinkedIn.com: The business person's social networking site

Facebook.com: Connect with friends and family and brand your business

Twitter.com: Short yet instant communication with industry bigwigs

YouTube.com: Broadcast yourself

BlogTalkRadio.com: Create your own online radio show

Mashable.com: Top source for news in social media, technology and web culture

Resources

Career-Success.ning.com: Interactive community for high performers

Socialmediatoday.com: Helping companies leverage the power of social media

Alltop.com: All the top stories

SocialMediaExaminer.com: Your guide to the social media jungle

WebWorkerDaily.com: Advice on how to use the web to be more productive, more connected and more successful

About the Author

Deborah Shane

Deborah Shane has successfully transformed herself from a rockin' singer and songwriter, teacher and award-winning broadcast radio sales professional into a gutsy entrepreneur as the leader of her own company, Train with Shane launched in 2006. In this exciting venture, Deborah has combined all of her skills and talents—entertainment, marketing, sales, mentoring, teaching and more—into a business that guides and motivates others through their career transition, business development and professional empowerment.

Each year Deborah reaches thousands of professionals through her offerings and has worked with a range of organizations, including businesses, professional organizations, schools, chambers, non-profits and government organizations.

Deborah has been featured in, quoted on and has contributed to a myriad of media, including Fox-TV, Careerealism.com, Smartbrief.com, Smallbiztrends. com, PersonalBrandingBlog.com, SparkandHustle. com and Job-Hunt.org.

Her blog, DeborahShaneToolbox.com, as well as her radio show, Deborah Shane's Metropolis, presents relevant, current topics on the new world of business and work, and the new way we live in it.

When she is not working, she's taking long bike rides, hiking to new heights, enjoying her family and friends, writing, traveling to cool places, loving all animals, and enjoying all arts and music.

Connect with Deborah Offline!

To book Deborah for..

Speaking | Events | Training |Consulting

www.DeborahShane.com

If you are struggling to find your passion and purpose..
If you want to make a career shift..
If you want to be successful at social marketing..
If you need to upgrade your professional skills..

Let Deborah GUIDE you on your new path!
By emPOWERing you to believe you can succeed!

Find out where Deborah's going to be for upcoming
speaking engagements, events and training at:
www.DeborahShane.com.

Drop by her website and send her a note,
she'd love to hear from you!

Connect and Engage with Deborah on her Web & Social Media Network!

www.twitter.com/deborahshane

www.facebook.com/deborahshane

www.linkedin.com/in/deborahshane

www.blogtalkradio.com/deborahshane

Deborah and other guest experts Blog weekly at:
www.deborahshanetoolbox.com

www.ingramcontent.com/pod-product-compliance
Lightning Source LLC
Chambersburg PA
CBHW051514170526
45165CB00002B/466